I0450467

RUSSIA'S DESTABILIZATION OF UKRAINE

HEARING

BEFORE THE

COMMITTEE ON FOREIGN AFFAIRS
HOUSE OF REPRESENTATIVES

ONE HUNDRED THIRTEENTH CONGRESS

SECOND SESSION

MAY 8, 2014

Serial No. 113–176

Printed for the use of the Committee on Foreign Affairs

Available via the World Wide Web: http://www.foreignaffairs.house.gov/ or
http://www.gpo.gov/fdsys/

U.S. GOVERNMENT PRINTING OFFICE

87–837PDF   WASHINGTON : 2014

COMMITTEE ON FOREIGN AFFAIRS

EDWARD R. ROYCE, California, *Chairman*

CHRISTOPHER H. SMITH, New Jersey
ILEANA ROS-LEHTINEN, Florida
DANA ROHRABACHER, California
STEVE CHABOT, Ohio
JOE WILSON, South Carolina
MICHAEL T. McCAUL, Texas
TED POE, Texas
MATT SALMON, Arizona
TOM MARINO, Pennsylvania
JEFF DUNCAN, South Carolina
ADAM KINZINGER, Illinois
MO BROOKS, Alabama
TOM COTTON, Arkansas
PAUL COOK, California
GEORGE HOLDING, North Carolina
RANDY K. WEBER SR., Texas
SCOTT PERRY, Pennsylvania
STEVE STOCKMAN, Texas
RON DeSANTIS, Florida
DOUG COLLINS, Georgia
MARK MEADOWS, North Carolina
TED S. YOHO, Florida
LUKE MESSER, Indiana

ELIOT L. ENGEL, New York
ENI F.H. FALEOMAVAEGA, American Samoa
BRAD SHERMAN, California
GREGORY W. MEEKS, New York
ALBIO SIRES, New Jersey
GERALD E. CONNOLLY, Virginia
THEODORE E. DEUTCH, Florida
BRIAN HIGGINS, New York
KAREN BASS, California
WILLIAM KEATING, Massachusetts
DAVID CICILLINE, Rhode Island
ALAN GRAYSON, Florida
JUAN VARGAS, California
BRADLEY S. SCHNEIDER, Illinois
JOSEPH P. KENNEDY III, Massachusetts
AMI BERA, California
ALAN S. LOWENTHAL, California
GRACE MENG, New York
LOIS FRANKEL, Florida
TULSI GABBARD, Hawaii
JOAQUIN CASTRO, Texas

AMY PORTER, *Chief of Staff*   THOMAS SHEEHY, *Staff Director*
JASON STEINBAUM, *Democratic Staff Director*

CONTENTS

RUSSIA'S DESTABILIZATION OF UKRAINE

THURSDAY, MAY 8, 2014

House of Representatives,
Committee on Foreign Affairs,
Washington, DC.

The committee met, pursuant to notice, at 10:10 a.m., in room 2172 Rayburn House Office Building, Hon. Edward Royce (chairman of the committee) presiding.

Chairman ROYCE. This committee will come to order. Despite the warnings issued and despite the sanctions imposed by the U.S. and our allies, we continue to see aggression against Ukraine. This is a crisis with violence intensifying. The presence of heavy weapons and the downing of Ukrainian helicopters betray the Kremlin's claim that it is not behind the unrest. Unfortunately, President Vladimir Putin appears to have calculated that the price will be bearable and this has to change.

The ranking member and I led a delegation to Ukraine last month where we heard loud and clear the desire for strong American leadership.

Fortunately, we have something to work with.

The Russian economy is weakening due to the Ukraine crisis. Russia's own Central Bank has said that $63.7 billion in capital has fled the country in the first quarter, a figure that the IMF predicts will reach $100 billion by the end of this year.

The Russian stock market, since the beginning of the year, has dropped 16 percent of its value and the ruble has also lost much of its value as interest rates have risen.

The World Bank has warned that Russia's growth rate this year could become negative. Much of this economic weakness is driven by the political risk of doing business in Russia.

Investors hate risk. We should do more to increase their risk perception if the Russian Government attempts to undermine the election on May 25th. That is a very important election.

We spent time in the eastern most part of Ukraine and the information that we received from talking to every group that we could access was that they were looking forward to the election. They felt the election would pull the country together.

I think there will be a big turnout on May 25th as long as it is not destabilized. We must stop reacting to Putin's moves while waiting patiently for the Europeans to join us.

Instead, we must adopt a proactive strategy that will convince President Putin that his aggression will have a significant and lasting cost to the Russian economy and ultimately to his rule should he intervene in that election.

We must also undermine Russia's ability to use its oil and gas exports to offset its economic weakness. Oil and gas make up over half of Russia's national budget. It is 52 percent of the support for the military and the government there. It is 70 percent of the exports.

President Putin understands that he is vulnerable to even small reductions in energy revenues.

To accomplish this longer-term goal of leverage, we must enhance energy efficiency in Ukraine and other countries that have traditionally depended on subsidized Russian energy exports in Eastern Europe.

We must assist European countries in developing their own energy resources. When we were there, we talked at length with the government in Ukraine about the ability to develop shale gas in the western part of that country and to bring new sources of energy to the European market, including through expediting the approval of LNG export facilities and ending the U.S. ban on crude oil exports.

Both in Poland and in Lithuania they are working on bringing online a receipt station for LNG by the end of the year and the reality is that they are very desirous, since we have a glut on our market, of having exports come from the United States into Eastern Europe. As you know, the Poles can directly flow that gas into Ukraine.

By allowing abundant U.S. energy resources to flow to Europe, we can help end energy dependency on Russia, helping to weaken Moscow's economic and political grip on its neighbors.

We must also expand and sharpen our international broadcasting to Russia and to Ukraine and others in the region in order to counter the propaganda that Moscow is peddling to spread instability and fear that it can then exploit. One of the most important things that can happen here is if we get back up on our feet with the type of effective broadcasting Radio Free Europe and Radio Liberty used to do into that part of the world. This committee just passed and the President signed legislation to improve broadcasting into Ukraine. We are in an information war and we are looking to see what else is needed in this effort to have surrogate radio bring real news in real time in terms of what is actually happening in the eastern part of the country and in Russia into that region.

It is essential that the U.S. reinforce our defense commitment to our NATO allies such as Poland and Lithuania, Latvia and Estonia to ensure that President Putin does not miscalculate and initiate a far more serious confrontation. But our NATO allies must take long overdue steps to increase their defense spending to 3 percent of GDP.

I feel that there are some real challenges here and I fear that our failure to match our warnings with equally strong action has undermined our credibility in some ways. It is my hope that we can restore our credibility by convincing President Putin that he is indeed risking his future in pursuit of objectives that are unworthy of a great nation.

I now turn to the ranking member, Mr. Eliot Engel of New York, for his remarks.

Mr. ENGEL. Well, thank you, Chairman Royce, for calling this hearing. The situation in Ukraine is one of the most urgent issues for American foreign policy. Madame Assistant Secretary and Mr. Assistant Secretary, thank you both for appearing before the committee today and thank you for your hard work in support of Ukraine.

I also want to acknowledge the presence here this morning of Ukrainian Ambassador Motsyk, who is in the audience. Welcome, Mr. Ambassador.

Right now, Ukrainian troops are battling separatists in Eastern Ukraine. The people of Odessa, the vibrant multi-cultural birthplace of one of my grandparents, are mourning those killed last weekend.

Tensions are high and there is a danger of further escalation in certain parts of the country. I want to express my condolences to the families of those who were killed.

It is clear that President Putin is responsible for this crisis. He has trampled on Ukraine's sovereignty. He has illegally seized Crimea, the first annexation in Europe since the end of World War II.

He has tried to instigate separatism and destabilize the country. He has massed his troops on Ukraine's border, promoted discord and conflict, and set individuals, families and peoples against one another.

Meanwhile, the people of Ukraine are trying to chart a new course for their country's future. The interim government in Kiev has done all it can to maintain stability and the Presidential election scheduled for May 25th gives Ukraine a path forward for a democratic return to political and economic health.

Chairman Royce and I, along with several other colleagues on this committee, recently visited Kiev. We heard the same thing over and over again. Ukrainians do not want Russian interference and they resent Russian attempts to tear their country apart.

The people of Ukraine are looking to us and our allies to ensure Putin's attempts to weaken their country do not succeed. The reality hit home for me when we visited a synagogue in Eastern Ukraine.

Two older men approached me to talk about the crisis. They had seen it all. They fought against Hitler's army in World War II to stop the spread of tyranny, only to find themselves living under the yoke of Soviet dictatorship for the next half century.

They saw the Wall crumble and felt the breeze of freedom and democracy blow across Eastern Europe and there, wearing the medals they had earned on the Ukrainian front, they were looking toward the east and seeing an all too familiar threat on the horizon.

''Don't abandon us,'' one of them said. Like so many others, those men want Ukraine to thrive in peace and prosperity. We need to have their backs. So President Putin must understand that his actions have consequences.

The White House did right by imposing targeted sanctions against individuals and companies associated with Putin and yesterday withdrawing Russia as a GSP beneficiary.

But if Russia continues to threaten and destabilize Ukraine we need to ratchet up the pressure further. We need stronger sanctions. I also call on our European partners and others around the world to work with us in imposing sanctions.

But sanctions will only be effective if they are part of a broader strategy on Ukraine and Russia. First, the best answer to Russian aggression is for Ukraine to become a fully democratic prosperous state. Wouldn't it be nice if Putin's aggression accelerated the process of democratization of Ukraine and made Ukraine look westward rather than eastward?

That is why I support robust international assistance including the U.S. and EU and centered on the IMF agreement to address Ukraine'simmediateeconomiccrisis.

Next, serious reform efforts—we should help Ukraine address structural economic weaknesses, combat corruption, secure its borders, rebuild its military, strengthen rule of law, and increase its energy security.

Secondly, to answer future threats from Russia, we need to focus on the role of a 21st century NATO. Even as NATO addresses challenges around the world, the alliance has to remain the guarantor of peace and security in Europe.

NATO allies, especially those on the eastern side of the alliance, must be confident that Article 5 guarantees remain in force. NATO needs to ramp up cooperative activities in Central Europe. We need to take a hard look at NATO's force posture and defensive assets in the region.

And most importantly, all 28 NATO allies need to live up to their responsibilities. Right now, only four countries devote at least 2 percent of their budgets to defense as they have committed to do by being a member of NATO.

If we increase NATO defense spending while joining in a coordinated embargo on all arms sales to Russia, including halting the sale of two French-built Mistral amphibious ships, it will send a clear message to Putin that he will not be allowed to trample on the rights of his neighbors.

On that note, I think the U.S. and our allies should work with Paris to find a way for NATO to purchase or lease these advanced warships to expand our capabilities while preventing their delivery to Moscow.

Third, in addition to helping Ukraine increase its energy security, we must urgently work with our European allies and others to reduce Europe's energy dependence on Russia.

And finally, we need to help ensure that the May 25th elections in Ukraine are safe, free and fair, and reflect the will of the people of Ukraine.

We hope that Ukraine's new President will begin the process of reconciliation by making clear that he or she represents all Ukrainians regardless of their regional, ethnic or religious identity.

Ukrainians need to work together to build a tolerant, pluralistic society. The new Ukrainian Government must be truly inclusive, support minority rights, and condemn all forms of intolerance.

As I heard repeatedly while in Ukraine, there is strong support for constitutional reforms and decentralization to give greater powers to regional and municipal authorities.

I want to emphasize that Ukraine's future is for Ukrainians alone to decide. At the same time, a lasting solution ensuring the stability of Ukraine requires Russia's cooperation.

So we must continue to talk with Russia and facilitate direct talks between Moscow and Kiev, including through international and regional fora such as the U.N. and OSCE.

I would like to close by again thanking our witnesses and the administration for all the work over the past several months to support democracy in Ukraine.

This is a very difficult time for Ukraine and it is important that its people know they have a friend in the United States. We support their country's sovereignty and territorial integrity and we support the aspirations of Ukrainians to build a better future for their country.

Thank you, Mr. Chairman.

Chairman ROYCE. Well, thank you, Mr. Engel. I do want to, again, thank Eliot Engel for his assistance on this CODEL and some of our other colleagues here as well—Lois Frankel, Alan Lowenthal, Judge Ted Poe, Mike Quigley, Jim Gerlach, David Cicilline. We appreciate the members of this committee and some of our other colleagues in the House for their engagement.

I now go for 2 minutes to Mr. Rohrabacher, chair of the Europe and Eurasia Subcommittee.

Mr. ROHRABACHER. Thank you, Mr. Chairman. I just happen to be chairman of this subcommittee at this particular moment in history. How interesting.

I think that we should all understand that the situation in Ukraine is much murkier than what is being presented by the rhetoric that we hear every day. This is not simply a case of Russian aggression.

This all began—when did this crisis begin? When did the chaos that we see begin? It began when an elected President of Ukraine, who was probably elected in the fairest and most honest election Ukraine has ever had, when that President, Yanukovych, was forced out of office by street violence. That is when this chaos started.

So let us not say, "Oh, my goodness, the Russians are responsible for this problem that is going on." The fact is it started before there was any Russian intervention at all when an elected President was thrown out and, my gosh, the United States didn't seem to be concerned that this elected person in a free election was being kicked out by what basically was based on street violence that created chaotic—a chaotic situation in which, of course, we ended up with what? And when was that street violence?

When did it start? It started when the elected President decided, as he rightfully was elected to do, to make an economic agreement with Russia rather than the EU.

No, this is much, much murkier than what is being presented. One thing is for sure. We should not be jumping into it. We should not be borrowing, and I am looking forward to the testimony of our witnesses today to find out exactly how much this is costing the American taxpayer.

When we are going into debt by hundreds of billions of dollars a year, for us to borrow more money in order to give it to Ukraine in situations like this doesn't make much sense. But I am anxious to hear what our witnesses have to say about how much this is costing the United States.

So with that, I thank the chairman for holding this hearing. I am interested in learning as much as I can and thank you very much, Mr. Chairman.

Chairman ROYCE. Thank you, Mr. Rohrabacher.

We now go for 2 minutes to Mr. Keating, the ranking member of the Europe, Eurasia, and Emerging Threats Subcommittee.

Mr. KEATING. Thank you, Mr. Chairman, and I would like to begin by thanking Assistant Secretary Nuland and Assistant Secretary Glaser for appearing today.

I have seen first hand, both in Europe and back home, how they and their teams of experts have been working overtime for the past 6 months to respond quickly and constantly to the changing situation in Ukraine.

Ambassador Pyatt and his team at the Embassy in Kiev merit special recognition for their heroic efforts. I am looking forward to hearing our witnesses' assessment of Russia's efforts to destabilize Ukraine's interim government and the effectiveness to date of U.S. sanctions.

Despite its April 17th pledge to help de-escalate the crisis in Ukraine, Russia has done exactly the opposite. There is nothing murky about that. It is clear as can be.

The role that Russian Special Services have played in destabilizing Eastern Ukraine is indisputable in supporting so-called separatists, coordinated armed attacks on government buildings, orchestrating kidnappings, and violence against local politicians, reporters, and even OSCE monitors.

Russian disinformation campaigns have only made matters worse and I echo the sentiments of the chairman of this committee as this committee has moved forward in a bipartisan effort to increase international broadcasting.

Russian forces' use of masked warfare and other covert tactics seems to signal a strategic shift in its approach to the region and to European security.

It is essential that the United States and NATO allies respond. I support the administration's decision to impose sanctions on individuals and entities closely linked to the Russian leadership's inner circle.

I also welcome the decision to impose export restrictions on key Russian companies and the additional restrictive measures on defense exports. The goal of these targeted sanctions is to send a clear signal that Russian aggression against Ukraine comes at a price.

I share the President's hope that these measures will persuade President Putin to reverse course. While President Putin's statement today is a hopeful sign, his true intentions remain unclear.

I am troubled by separatists' insistence that they move ahead with a referendum this weekend and I therefore fully support the administration's readiness to impose additional penalties if Russia continues to press forward, including targeted sanctions against specific sectors of the Russian economy.

As the United States moves forward, it is imperative that we do so in coordination with our European allies and I look forward to hearing about the status of the administration's ongoing discussions with the EU as well as efforts within NATO to counter Russian aggression and reassure our Central European and Baltic allies.

With that, I yield back, Mr. Chairman.

Chairman ROYCE. I thank the gentleman. This morning we are pleased to be joined by representatives of the Department of State and the Department of the Treasury.

Ms. Victoria Nuland. Before assuming her position as Assistant Secretary for the Bureau of European and Eurasian Affairs at the Department of State, she served as the Department of State's spokesperson.

She also served as the United States Permanent Representative to the North Atlantic Treaty Organization from 2005 to 2008, focusing heavily on NATO-Russia issues, among other distinguished roles.

Mr. Daniel Glaser. Prior to his confirmation as Assistant Secretary for Terrorist Financing in the Office of Terrorism and Financial Intelligence in the Department of the Treasury, he served as the first director of the Treasury's Executive Office of Terrorist Financing and Financial Crimes and was an attorney for the U.S. Secret Service. We worked with Mr. Glaser some years ago because he was heavily involved in U.S. efforts to target North Korea with financial sanctions when he caught them in the act of counterfeiting $100 bills in Macao.

Macao was laundering the bills from North Korea into the financial system and the sanctions put on that bank and 10 other banks until they were lifted by the Department of State were particularly effective in stopping hard currency flows into North Korea.

Without objection, the witnesses' full prepared statement will be made part of the record. Members will have 5 calendar days to submit statements and questions, extraneous materials for the record if you wish.

And Ambassador Nuland, if you would, please summarize your remarks to 5 minutes and then we will go to Mr. Glaser and then to questions.

STATEMENT OF THE HONORABLE VICTORIA NULAND, ASSISTANT SECRETARY, BUREAU OF EUROPEAN AND EURASIAN AFFAIRS, U.S. DEPARTMENT OF STATE

Ms. NULAND. Thank you, Chairman Royce, Ranking Member Engel, members of this committee for inviting us today. As you said, Mr. Chairman, I have submitted a far more detailed statement for the record.

Let me begin by expressing my gratitude for the strong bipartisan engagement of this committee in support of Ukraine and its people. Your passage of the U.S. loan guarantee legislation demonstrated the American people's commitment to help Ukraine at this critical time, and your visits to Kiev and to Dnipropetrovsk reinforce America's solidarity with Ukrainian people and made an enormous impact on the ground. So thank you to all of you who travelled and to the bipartisan leadership of this committee.

Today, I want to outline four pillars of U.S. policy to address the challenges that we face in Ukraine. First, the United States is supporting Ukraine with financial, technical, and non-lethal security assistance as it prepares for the democratic Presidential elections on May 25th and we agree with you, Mr. Chairman, these are absolutely the most vital elections Ukraine has had in recent history.

Second, we are working with Ukraine and our European partners to leave the door open for diplomatic de-escalation should Russia change course and make a serious effort to implement its April 17 Geneva commitments.

Third, we are steadily raising the economic costs for Russia's occupation and illegal annexation of Crimea and any continuing efforts to destabilize eastern and southern Ukraine.

And fourth, we are stepping up our efforts to reassure our NATO allies. So let me go through them quickly.

First, in addition to the $1 billion loan guarantee approved on April 1st, the United States is providing $178 million in Fiscal Year '13 and '14 State and AID funds, plus an additional $50 million in technical assistance to support programs to maintain macroeconomic stability, to advance anti-corruption reform, to mitigate the vulnerability of Ukraine to outside economic pressure, especially from Russia, and especially in the energy sector, and to support energy efficiency, and to recover stolen assets of the Ukrainian state and the Ukrainian people.

We are also providing more than $18 million in non-lethal security assistance to the Ukrainian armed forces and the state border guard service. Our $11 million in electoral assistance supports efforts at voter education and civic participation.

It assists the Central Electoral Commission to administer the elections effectively and transparently. It supports election security, which will be absolutely essential, and it guarantees a diverse, balanced, and policy-focused media.

We are also supporting 255 long-term local observers and over 3,300 short-term observers. In addition, we are working with the OSCE's Office of Democratic Institutions and Human Rights, ODIHR, as they prepare to deploy 1,000 observers throughout the country monitoring the elections, the largest monitoring effort in ODIHR's history.

Second, along with our allies and the international community we remain committed to a diplomatic de-escalation should that be possible. As you know, on April 17th in Geneva the United States, Ukraine, Russia and the EU came together to develop a blueprint for such de-escalation.

At its core, the Geneva joint statement was and remains a grand bargain that offered amnesty for those who vacate seized buildings plus deep, broad decentralization of power to Ukraine's regions through national dialogue and constitutional reform in parallel with an end to violence, intimidation, and the seizure of buildings and weapons.

As you know, the Ukrainian Government began implementing its part of the Geneva agreement even before the ink was dry on the text. The day after the Ukrainian Government sent a draft amnesty bill to the Rada. Within a week, Ukrainian authorities had dismantled barricades in Kiev and opened streets.

On April 14th, 29th, and just yesterday, the Constitutional Reform Commission has held broad public conferences with all the regions and Ukrainian security forces instituted an Easter pause in their operations and sent senior officials out with the OSCE teams to Donetsk and Slovyansk and Luhansk and other embattled cities to try to talk separatists into pursuing their aims politically, rather than through violence.

And you will have seen the trip of Prime Minister Yatsenyuk to the most embattled area of the east Slovyansk yesterday on a mission of political reconciliation.

In contrast, Russia has fulfilled none of its commitments. The separatists in Donetsk and Luhansk told OSCE observers that they hadn't even received any messages at all from Russia urging them to stand down.

Yesterday was in fact the first time we heard President Putin call for the illegally armed groups to stand down. Instead, since April 17th all of the efforts of Ukraine and the OSCE have been met with more violence, more mayhem, kidnappings, torture and death.

As Secretary Kerry has stated, we continue to have high confidence that Russia's hand is behind this instability. And yet Russia can still step back from supporting separatism and violence.

Today, we are working closely with the Government of Ukraine, with the OSCE, with key European governments including Germany, to once again support a diplomatic path forward—a rejuvenation, if you will, of the Geneva commitments.

We do consider it a positive step that President Putin yesterday spoke out in opposition to the proposed May 11th separatist referendum in Donetsk and Luhansk.

Now what we hope to see is Moscow completely end its support for separatists altogether and actively encourage an end to building occupations, disarmament of illegal groups, and the healing of Ukraine through the political process. That means Presidential elections, national dialogue on broad constitutional reform through decentralization.

This is the peaceful path forward, and we will judge Russia's sincerity by its actions in the coming days, not by its words.

This brings me to the third pillar of our strategy. In response to Russia's continued occupation of Crimea and its aggressive acts in east and south Ukraine, the United States has imposed significant costs on Russia.

Just last week we enacted new sanctions on seven Russian Government officials including two members of Putin's inner circle and 17 entities.

Assistant Secretary Glaser will go into the details, and as the President made clear last week we are prepared to exact a higher cost if Russia takes further steps to destabilize Ukraine, including disrupting the May 25th elections, and we are working now with our European and global partners on a package of sectoral sanctions that will bite quite deeply into the Russian economy, if we have to use them.

The Russian economy, as you said, Mr. Chairman, is already buckling under the pressure of these internationally imposed sanctions. Its credit ratings are hovering just above junk status.

Fifty one billion in capital has fled Russia since the beginning of the year, which is close to the $60 billion they lost in all of 2013. Russian bonds are trading at higher yields than any debt in Europe and as the ruble has fallen, the Central Bank has raised interest rates twice and has spent close to $30 billion from its reserves since early March to try to prop up the ruble.

And finally, our fourth pillar—we are working intensively with our NATO allies to provide visible reassurance on land, on sea, and in the air that Article 5 of the NATO treaty means what it says. Our message to Russia is clear: NATO territory is inviolable. We will defend every piece of it and we are mounting a visible deterrent to any Russian efforts to test that.

The United States, as you know, has increased our own contribution to NATO Baltic air policing. We have bolstered the U.S.-Poland aviation detachment at Lask Air Force Base and we have maintained a steady U.S. naval presence in the Black Sea. We have also deployed a total of 750 U.S. ground troops to Estonia, Latvia, Lithuania, Poland and Romania.

We are now heartened that more than half of the other NATO allies have also offered visible reassurance contributions to the NATO mission to support the front line states, including increased air and land reassurances by the U.K., France, Canada and Germany and reassurances at sea from Norway, Belgium, the Netherlands and Estonia.

Taken together, these four pillars of our policy—support for Ukraine, costs for Russia, an open door for de-escalation through diplomacy, and allied reassurance—are the foundation of the work we are doing together and with this committee and with the Congress.

In this effort, we appreciate your bipartisan support and your bipartisan contribution and we hope to continue to work closely with you.

Thank you.

[The prepared statement of Ms. Nuland follows:]

Victoria Nuland
Assistant Secretary of State for European and Eurasian Affairs
House Foreign Affairs Committee
May 8, 2014
Written Testimony

Chairman Royce, Ranking Member Engel, thank you for inviting me to testify today on our efforts to counter Russia's de-stabilizing, provocative actions in Ukraine and to preserve Ukraine as a united, democratic state.

Let me begin by expressing my gratitude for the strong bipartisan engagement of this committee in the crisis that has engulfed Ukraine and its people. Your passage of the U.S. loan guarantee legislation provided the United States with authority for a key element of our assistance. And the visits that many of you have made to Ukraine, most recently led by Chairman Royce to Kyiv and Dnipropetrovsk, reinforce America's solidarity with the Ukrainian people during this critical time.

Today I want to outline four pillars of U.S. policy to address the challenges facing Ukraine. First, the United States is supporting Ukraine with financial, technical and non-lethal security assistance as it prepares for democratic presidential elections on May 25th, and works to protect a peaceful, secure, prosperous and unified future for its people. Second, we are working with Ukraine and our European partners to leave the door open for diplomatic de-escalation should Russia change course, and make a serious effort to implement its April 17 Geneva commitments. Third, we are steadily raising the economic costs for Russia's occupation and illegal annexation of Crimea and its continuing efforts to destabilize eastern and southern Ukraine; Assistant Secretary Glaser will address the sanctions we've imposed and what's next. And fourth, we are stepping up our effort to reassure our NATO allies and we are providing support to other frontline states like Moldova and Georgia.

First, the U.S. is providing assistance to Ukraine in areas in which it needs it most. In addition to $92 million in FY2013 State/USAID funds and $86 million in FY2014 funds, we are providing an additional $50 million in technical assistance and the $1 billion dollar loan guarantee under the authority passed by Congress on April 1st. This support is vital to Ukraine's efforts to administer the presidential elections successfully on May 25th. The best rebuke to violent separatism is a free, fair election across Ukraine in which average citizens confirm their faith in achieving these goals politically rather than through the barrel of a gun and place Ukraine on the path that its people want and deserve.

Our electoral assistance aims to improve the integrity of the election process. We have allocated $11 million for non-partisan election activities, including efforts to support voter education and civic participation; assist the Central Electoral Commission to administer the elections effectively and transparently; foster linkages between political parties and civil society; support election security; and help to guarantee a diverse, balanced and policy-focused media environment. In addition to the 100 OSCE observers we are sending, the United States is supporting 255 long-term observers and over 3300 short-term observers, along with a parallel vote tabulation (PVT) process.

In addition, we are working multilaterally with the OSCE's Office for Democratic Institutions and Human Rights (ODIHR) as it prepares to deploy 1,000 observers throughout the country to monitor the elections—the largest monitoring effort in the Organization's history. The United States will provide approximately one tenth of the observers, and 26 other OSCE states are also contributing. These 1,000 ODIHR observers will be joined by more than 100 members of the OSCE Parliamentary Assembly, including some of your colleagues here on the Hill.

More broadly, we are assisting Ukraine with financial and technical assistance to maintain macroeconomic stability, recover stolen assets from overseas, advance anti-corruption reform, and mitigate vulnerability to economic pressure from Russia, especially in the energy sector. And we are providing more than $18 million in non-lethal security assistance to the Ukrainian armed forces and State Border Guard Service to enable them to fulfill their core missions. And we continue to work with Ukraine to determine their requirements and review options to provide additional security assistance.

Second, along with our allies and the international community, we remain committed to de-escalation and a diplomatic off-ramp should Russia choose to take it. On April 17th in Geneva, the United States, Ukraine, Russia, and the EU came together to develop a blueprint for de-escalation. At its core, the Geneva Joint Statement was and remains a grand bargain: it offers amnesty for those who vacate seized buildings plus deep, broad decentralization of power to Ukraine's regions through national dialogue and constitutional reform in parallel with an end to violence, intimidation, and the seizure of buildings and weapons.

The Ukrainian government began implementing its part of Geneva even before the ink was dry on the text of the Joint Statement. The day after Geneva, the government of Ukraine sent a draft amnesty bill to the Rada. Within a week, authorities in Kyiv had dismantled barricades and opened streets. Maidan activists peacefully vacated the Kyiv city administration building. On April 14th and 29th, the constitutional reform commission held public conferences to which all the regions were invited. Ukrainian security forces instituted an Easter pause in their operations in eastern Ukraine, and sent senior officials out with the OSCE teams to Donetsk, Slovyansk, Luhansk and other embattled cities to try to talk separatists into pursuing their aims politically rather than through violence.

In contrast, Russia fulfilled none of its commitments. After we left Geneva, no one in Moscow at any level even issued a public statement calling for buildings and checkpoints in eastern Ukraine to be vacated and weapons turned in. Russia declined a request by the OSCE to send senior representatives to eastern Ukraine to insist on separatist implementation of Geneva. In fact, separatists in Donetsk and Luhansk told OSCE observers that they had had no messages at all from Russia urging them to stand down. Yesterday was, in fact, the first time we heard President Putin call for illegally armed groups to stand down.

Instead, since April 17th, all the efforts of the Ukrainian side and of the OSCE have been met with more violence, mayhem, kidnappings, torture and death. Pro-Russia separatists have seized at least 35 buildings and 3 TV/radio centers in 24 towns. Armed and organized Russian agents – sometimes described as "little green men" – appeared in cities and towns across Donetsk and into Luhansk. At least 22 kidnappings have been attributed to pro-Russia separatists – including the 8 Vienna Document inspectors and their Ukrainian escorts who were released after 8 days as hostages. The bodies of three Ukrainians were found near Slovyansk all bearing the signs of torture. Peaceful rallies have been beset by armed separatist thugs. Roma families have fled Slovyansk under extreme duress. As the violence grew, the United States and the EU imposed more sanctions at the end of April. Last Friday, the Ukrainian government announced that separatists used MANPADs to shoot down a Ukrainian helicopter, killing the pilots. And Friday also saw the deadliest tragedy of this conflict: the death of more than 40 in Odesa following violent clashes reportedly instigated by pro-Russian separatists attacking an initially peaceful rally in favor of national unity.

Russia claims it has "no influence" over the separatists and provocateurs rampaging in eastern and southern Ukraine. It should come as no surprise that, in Odesa, the Ukrainian authorities report that those arrested for igniting the violence included people whose papers indicate that they come from Transnistria, the Crimea region of Ukraine, and Russia. As Secretary Kerry has stated, we continue to have high confidence that Russia's hand is behind this instability. They are providing material support. They are providing funding. They are providing weapons. They are providing coordination, and there are Russians agents on the ground in Ukraine involved in this.

Equally worrying, today from Slovyansk to Odesa the playbook is identical to what we saw in Crimea: first you create upheaval in towns that were completely peaceful just 2 months before, then you intimidate the local population, and hold bogus independence referenda on 2 weeks' notice, as have been declared for May 11 in the so-called Donetsk and Luhansk Peoples' Republics. In this regard, we consider it a positive step that

President Putin spoke out yesterday in opposition to the proposed May 11th referendum, which would have been illegal and illegitimate.

Russia can still step back from supporting separatism and violence and do the right thing. Working closely with the Ukrainians, the OSCE, and key European governments including Germany, we are once again supporting a diplomatic path forward – a rejuvenation of the Geneva commitments: amnesty for separatists and real political reform through elections and constitutional change in exchange for the peace, security and unity across Ukraine that these require. A Russia that truly cares about the fate of the ethnic Russians in Ukraine and the people of eastern Ukraine will work with us on this. A Russia that doesn't will face a tightening grip of political and economic isolation from the international community.

Which brings me to the third pillar of our strategy: In response to Russia's cynical and aggressive ploy in eastern Ukraine— and continued occupation of Crimea— the U.S. has imposed significant costs on Russia. Last week, the U.S. enacted new sanctions on seven Russian government officials, including two members of President Putin's inner circle, and 17 entities. Further, we have tightened export licenses for any high-technology items that could contribute to Russia's military capabilities. A/S Glaser will speak to this in further detail. The President made clear last week that we are prepared to exact a higher cost if Russia takes further steps to destabilize Ukraine including disrupting the May 25th elections.

The Russian economy is already buckling under the pressure of these internationally imposed sanctions. Its credit rating is hovering just above "junk" status. $51 billion in capital has fled Russia since the beginning of the year, approaching the $60 billion figure for all of 2013. Russian bonds are trading at higher yields than any debt in Europe. As the ruble has fallen, the Central Bank has raised interest rates twice and has spent close to $30 billion from its reserves since early March to stabilize it.

Finally, we have worked with our NATO Allies to provide visible reassurance—on land, sea and in the air—that Article 5 of the NATO Treaty means what it says. Our message to Putin and Russia is clear: as the President said on March 20, "America's support for our NATO allies is unwavering. We are bound together by our profound Article 5 commitment to defend one another. . ." As a result, the United States has increased our contribution to NATO's Baltic Air Policing mission. We have bolstered the U.S.-Poland aviation training detachment in Lask, Poland with 12 F-16s and 200 personnel. We have maintained a steady U.S. naval presence in the Black Sea. And the United States has deployed a total of 750 troops to Estonia, Latvia, Lithuania, Poland and Romania.

And we are heartened that more than half of the other NATO Allies have also offered visible reassurance on the frontline. The U.K. and France are sending fighter jets to

NATO's Baltic Air Policing mission and Germany will participate beginning in September. The U.K. and Canada are sending ground troops to take part in exercises. And Norway, Belgium, the Netherlands and Estonia are participating in a naval countermine group in the Baltic. We are encouraging other Allies to step up, and all Allies to do more.

Taken together, these four pillars—support for Ukraine, costs for Russia, an open door for de-escalation through diplomacy and Allied reassurance— are the foundation of America's response to this crisis. In this effort, we appreciate Congress's bipartisan support and will continue work in close coordination with you on all of these areas.

Thank you and I look forward to your questions.

———————

Chairman ROYCE. Mr. Glaser.

STATEMENT OF THE HONORABLE DANIEL GLASER, ASSIST-ANT SECRETARY, OFFICE OF TERRORISM AND FINANCIAL INTELLIGENCE, U.S. DEPARTMENT OF THE TREASURY

Mr. GLASER. Thank you, Chairman Royce, and thank you for that kind introduction. I am going to go off script just for a second to thank you for calling the work that we did together in 2005, 2006, 2007, that really was the proof of concept that it is possible to apply targeted financial measures in a strategic way against a target and we learned a lot from that and we have really taken off since then and it was a pleasure working with you back then. I look forward——

Chairman ROYCE. I just wish we had done it again, Mr. Glaser.

Mr. GLASER. Well, we are doing our best, Mr. Chairman. But to my remarks, Chairman Royce, Ranking Member Engel, distinguished members of the committee, thank you for inviting me to speak today about the U.S. Government's response to Russia's illegal annexation of Crimea and its continued provocative actions in Ukraine.

The Department of the Treasury is designing and implementing a strategy that uses targeted financial measures to raise the costs to Russia of its actions.

Our approach is calibrated to impose immediate costs on Russia and to create conditions that will make Russia increasingly vulnerable to sanctions as the situation in Ukraine escalates.

To this end, Treasury has targeted not only corrupt former Ukrainian officials, Crimean separatists and their backers in the Russian Government, but individuals in President Putin's inner circle who have important interests and holdings throughout the Russian economy.

Russia is already feeling the impact of our measures. In my remarks today, I will describe Treasury's sanctions tools and how we are deploying them. I will also discuss the important measures we are taking to buttress the Ukrainian economy.

By pursuing these dual tracks, the Treasury Department is using the tools at our disposal to contribute to the development of a strong and sovereign Ukraine.

President Obama has signed three Executive orders that provide the Secretary of the Treasury with expanded authority to sanction individuals responsible for the continuation of the crisis in Ukraine as well as entities under their control. In total, we have designated 45 individuals and 19 entities over four traunches of designations.

The most important of these targets include those in Putin's inner circle and the companies they control or own. These include Igor Sechin, the chairman of the state-run oil company Rosneft, Sergei Chemezov, the CEO of the Russian weapons and metals conglomerate Rostec, and Gennady Timchenko, who runs Gunvor, one of the world's largest commodity trading firms.

We have also targeted Russian officials directing the annexation of Crimea as well as Crimean separatists and former Ukrainian Government officials.

We have a range of options we can deploy should Russia's leadership continue to destabilize Ukraine. For example, Treasury has additional authority authorized by President Obama under Executive Order 13662 to significantly enhance Russia's economic costs in isolation.

This Executive order authorizes the targeting of entities operating in broad sectors of the Russian economy such as defense, metals, mining, finance, engineering, and energy.

I should note the importance of coordination with our international partners, particularly those in the European Union and the G–7. To be clear, the United States always stands ready to take actions we deem necessary to safeguard our national security and to safeguard international security.

We do, however, recognize that our financial measures are more powerful and effective when done in a multilateral framework.

Our partners have taken sanctions measures of their own and they have started to prepare to do more. We are working to ensure that our international partners continue and expand their measures, and that we move forward together to address Russia's aggression.

For example, this week Under Secretary David Cohen is leading an interagency delegation in Europe to coordinate precisely this, going to stops such as London, Paris and Berlin.

But even as we lay the groundwork for expanded measures if necessary, our sanctions are having an impact on Russia's already weak economy, and actually Chairman Royce rattled off most of the numbers that I have to rattle off.

But I will do it again because I do think they bear repeating. As sanctions increase, the costs to Russia will not only increase but their ability to mitigate the costs that they incur will diminish.

Already market analysts are forecasting significant continued outflows of both foreign and domestic capital and a further weakening of growth prospects for the year. The Russian stock market has declined over 13 percent and the Russian currency has depreciated by almost 8 percent since the beginning of the year, the worst numbers within the group of emerging markets.

The IMF has downgraded Russia's growth outlook to .2 percent this year. That is the second downgrade within a month and they have suggested that a recession is not out of the question.

This stands in stark contrast to previous IMF forecasts, which as recently as February were projecting 2 percent growth for Russia. The IMF also indicated that they expect as much as $100 billion in capital flight from Russia this year, which has caused rating agencies such as Standard & Poors to downgrade Russia's sovereign credit rating to just above junk status.

In addition to our measures that isolate the Russian economy, the Department of the Treasury is working with the international community to support the Ukrainian Government in returning the country's economy to solid footing.

As an important first step, Ukraine received the first traunch of $3 billion from the IMF—from the IMF's 2-year $17 billion reform package with an additional $3 billion expected to be disbursed by the end of May.

Treasury is also offering its expertise in identifying, tracking, and recovering stolen Ukrainian assets in support of Department of Justice efforts. Expert Treasury advisers have also been deployed to Kiev to help the Ukrainian authorities stabilize the financial sector and implement reforms.

As the United States and our international partners continue to confront Russia's illegal actions in Ukraine, we stand ready to further employ our arsenal of financial measures as the situation escalates.

A diplomatic resolution of the crisis remains our goal, but if Russia chooses to continue its illegal and destabilizing actions in Ukraine, we can impose substantial costs on and expand the isolation of an already weak Russian economy.

Thank you for the opportunity to speak today and I will be happy to answer your questions.

[The prepared statement of Mr. Glaser follows:]

Testimony of Assistant Secretary Daniel L. Glaser
House Committee on Foreign Affairs
Russia's Destabilization of Ukraine
Thursday, May 8, 2014

Chairman Royce, Ranking Member Engel, and distinguished Members of this Committee, thank you for inviting me to speak today about the U.S. Government's response to Russia's illegal annexation of Crimea and its continued provocative actions in Ukraine. The Department of the Treasury is designing and implementing a strategy that uses our toolkit of targeted financial measures to raise the costs to Russia of its actions. Our approach is a calibrated effort to impose immediate costs on Russia and to create conditions that will make Russia increasingly vulnerable to sanctions as the situation in Ukraine escalates. To this end, Treasury has targeted not only corrupt former Ukrainian officials, Crimean separatists, and their backers in the Russian government, but also individuals in President Putin's inner circle who have important interests and holdings throughout the Russian economy. Russia is already feeling the impact of our measures. As the Kremlin's decisions concerning the situation in Ukraine leave us with little choice but to continue to ratchet up the pressure, we will use the full range of sanctions authorities at our disposal, which will expose the weakness and vulnerability of the Russian economy.

In my remarks today I will describe Treasury's sanctions tools and how we are deploying them. I will also discuss the important measures we are taking to buttress the Ukrainian economy. By pursuing these dual tracks of imposing significant costs on Russia's illegal and destabilizing actions and facilitating the institution of the economic conditions necessary for a vibrant and prosperous Ukrainian economy, the Treasury Department is using the tools at our disposal to contribute to the development of a strong and sovereign Ukraine.

Imposing Costs on Russia: Sanctions and Financial Isolation

President Obama has signed three Executive Orders that provide the Secretary of the Treasury with expanded authority to sanction individuals and entities responsible for the continuation of the crisis in Ukraine, as well as entities owned or controlled by such individuals. These Executive Orders are as follows:

- E.O. 13660 provides the authority to block the assets of any individuals or entities determined to be responsible for or complicit in undermining democratic processes or institutions in Ukraine; threatening the peace, security, stability, sovereignty, or territorial integrity of Ukraine; misappropriating Ukrainian state assets; asserting governmental authority over any part of Ukraine, without authorization from the Government of Ukraine; or providing material assistance to any individual or entity that does;

- E.O. 13661 provides the authority to block the assets of any individuals or entities determined to be an official of the Russian government; operating in the arms sector in Russia; or providing material assistance to, or acting on behalf of, a senior official of the Russian government; or providing material assistance to any individual or entity whose assets are blocked;

- E.O. 13662 provides the authority to block the assets of any individuals or entities determined to be operating in such sectors of the Russian Federation economy as may be determined by the Secretary of the Treasury, in consultation with the Secretary of State, such as financial services, energy, metals and mining, engineering, and defense and related materiel; or providing material assistance to any individual or entity that does.

As noted above, we are implementing these Executive Orders in the context of a pressure strategy designed to impose immediate costs on Russia, including at high levels in Moscow, and to create market conditions that will make Russia increasingly vulnerable to financial measures and accountable as the situation in Ukraine escalates. In total we have imposed sanctions on 45 individuals and 19 entities to date. Our targets can be organized into the following categories:

Targeting Putin's Inner Circle and Certain Related Companies

- Igor Sechin, the Chairman of the State-run oil company Rosneft, and close associate of Putin;

- Sergei Chemezov, a trusted ally of Putin, who is also the CEO of the Russian weapons and metals conglomerate Rostec;

- Gennady Timchenko, who at the time of the designation ran Gunvor, one of the world's largest commodities trading firms, the funds of which may have been accessible to President Putin. Treasury also designated Timchenko's Volga Group, one of the largest investment groups in Russia, and Stroytransgaz Holding, an engineering and construction company for Russia's oil and gas industry, also controlled by Timchenko;

- The Rotenberg brothers, Arkady and Boris, who were designated for their role in supporting Putin's personal projects by receiving and executing high-price contracts for the Sochi Olympics and for state-controlled energy giant Gazprom. We also designated firms under the Rotenberg's control, including banks InvestCapitalBank and SMP Bank, as well as a gas pipeline company, SGM Group;

- Yuri Kovalchuk, who served as the personal banker for Putin and many senior Russian officials, earning the moniker "Putin's cashier"; and

- Treasury designated Bank Rossiya for its close connections to Putin's inner circle and the fact that it is controlled by the inner circle's personal banker Kovalchuk. Before sanctions were imposed, Bank Rossiya was among the 20 largest banks in Russia, with approximately $10 billion in assets. As a result of our designation, Bank Rossiya lost almost $1 billion in deposits in March and was forced to sell almost $500 million worth of bonds to maintain liquidity. The bank has also lost access to its correspondent accounts in U.S. financial institutions, and we are in close cooperation with our European and global partners to ensure that other financial centers do not provide services to this bank.

Targeting Russian Officials Directing the Purported Annexation of Crimea

Our efforts have also targeted Russian officials in response to the illegal annexation of Crimea. These officials include senior Duma and Federation council officials, such as the Speaker and Deputy Duma Speaker, key Duma deputies, and senior leaders in the Federation Council. Treasury has also imposed sanctions on senior Kremlin aides, including the Chief of Staff of the Presidential Executive Office, Advisor to the President, and Head of the Presidential Administration, as well as other senior Russian government officials, including the Head of the Russian Military Intelligence Service, the Chairman of the Board of Russian Railways, Director of the Federal Drug Control Service, and Director of Russia's Protective Service.

Targeting Crimean Separatists and Former Ukrainian Government Officials

We have also identified Crimean separatists and former Ukrainian government officials for their involvement in the illegal referendum on Crimean secession and purported annexation by Russia. These include Viktor Yanukovych, who, along with his regime's cohorts, was responsible for actions that threaten the security, stability, sovereignty, or territorial integrity of Ukraine, the self-appointed "Prime Minster of Crimea" Sergei Aksyonov, Vladimir Konstantinov the speaker of the Crimean Parliament, and Viktor Medvedchuk, a political party leader responsible for pitting supporters and foes of Russia's attempt to annex Crimea against one another.

As noted above, President Obama has given the Secretary of the Treasury additional authority to significantly enhance Russia's economic costs and isolation. Executive Order 13662 authorizes the targeting of individuals and entities operating in broad sectors of the Russian economy to be identified by the Secretary of the Treasury, in consultation with the Secretary of State, such as defense, metals and mining, finance, engineering, and energy. Treasury has been working closely with our colleagues within the U.S. Government, and with counterparts within the European Union and G-7, to design a strategy to deploy our full range of tools to target the Russian economy should Russia's leadership continue to destabilize Ukraine, including by attempting to disrupt this month's Presidential election.

In this regard, I should note the importance of coordination with our international partners, particularly those in the European Union and G-7. To be clear, the United States always stands ready to take the actions we deem necessary to safeguard international security. We do, however, recognize that our financial measures are more powerful and effective when done in a multilateral framework. This is certainly the case in the context of Russia, which is financially and economically integrated with Europe and the G-7 countries to a significant degree. Our partners have taken sanctions measures of their own, and have stated that they are prepared to do more should circumstances require. It will be important for them to do so, and the State and Treasury Departments are working tirelessly to ensure that our international partners continue and expand their measures as we move forward together to address Russia's efforts to destabilize Ukraine.

Impact: The Costs of Sanctions on the Russian Economy

Sanctions, and the uncertainty they have created in the market, are having an impact, directly and indirectly, on Russia's weak economy. And as sanctions increase, the costs will not only increase, but Russia's ability to mitigate costs will diminish. Already, market analysts are forecasting significant continued outflows of both foreign and domestic capital and a further weakening of growth prospects for the year. The IMF has downgraded Russia's growth outlook to 0.2 percent this year, and suggested that recession is not out of the question. This stands in stark contrast to previous IMF forecasts, which as recently as February were projecting 2 percent growth. It is clear that our sanctions policy is working:

- Since the start of the year, Russia's stock market has declined by over 13 percent;

- The Russian ruble has depreciated by almost 8 percent since the beginning of the year, despite substantial market intervention by the Russian Central Bank and an interest rate hike, amid heavy capital outflows that have already exceed last year's total;

- The Central Bank of Russia has spent nearly $50 billion (10 percent of its total foreign exchange reserves) in an effort to defend the value of the ruble;

- The yield on Russia's 10-year government bond is up over 170 basis points;

- The government is feeling the bite of rising borrowing costs. On April 23, Russia was forced to cancel a debt auction due to a spike in the price investors demanded to buy Russian bonds;

- IMF expects as much as $100 billion in capital flight from Russia this year; the World Bank puts that estimate closer to $130 billion;

- Citing recent large capital outflows and a deteriorating economic outlook, S&P downgraded Russia's sovereign credit rating to BBB-, or one notch above junk status, with a negative outlook; and

- S&P has downgraded ratings and outlook for several Russian banks and corporations on the deteriorating outlook for the Russian economy.

Supporting Ukraine

In addition to our measures to isolate the Russian economy, the Department of the Treasury is working with the international community to support the Ukrainian government in returning the country's economy to solid footing. Last week's approval of a two-year, $17 billion IMF reform program is a positive first step and has unlocked additional bilateral and multilateral financial support to help Ukraine as it undertakes essential reforms to set its economy on the path to sustainable growth.

The IMF will be at the center of this international assistance effort and is best placed to support Ukraine's implementation of robust and market-oriented reforms. The Ukrainian authorities have already begun undertaking the necessary steps to build a secure economic foundation, including urgently needed market reforms that will restore financial stability, improve economic potential, and allow Ukraine's people to better achieve their economic aspirations.

Total financial support from the international community for Ukraine is expected to reach $27 billion over the next two years, including support from the IMF, World Bank, European Bank for Reconstruction and Development, European Investment Bank, the United States, European Union, Canada, Japan, and possibly other bilateral donors. Financial support for Ukraine totaling $5.9 billion is estimated to be released in May, including $3.2 billion from the IMF and an estimated $2.7 billion from the United States, EU, World Bank, Japan, and Canada.

Our $1 billion loan guarantee agreement with the Ukrainians was signed last month, and we continue to work expeditiously to enable Ukraine to issue the $1 billion in U.S. guaranteed debt by mid-May – the proceeds of which will allow the Ukrainian government to insulate vulnerable Ukrainians from the impact of necessary economic reforms.

In addition to this direct financial support, the international community is supporting Ukrainian efforts to recover billions of dollars in assets stolen by the former Yanukovych regime. At an international conference last week in London, Attorney General Holder announced that the FBI would form a "financial SWAT team" to assist the Ukrainian government. In support of this effort, Treasury will offer its expertise in identifying, tracking, and recovering stolen Ukrainian state assets, following the Department of Justice's lead. Already, Treasury's Financial Crimes Enforcement Network (FinCEN) issued an advisory on February 26 reminding U.S. financial institutions of their responsibility to apply enhanced scrutiny to private banking accounts of assets related to Viktor Yanukovych. When the Ukrainian government announced its criminal investigation against Yanukovych officials for misappropriation of state assets, we added those names to the list to be scrutinized as well.

The United States has also pledged $50 million for new programs to address emerging needs in Ukraine. As a part of these efforts, expert Treasury advisors have been deployed to Kyiv to help the Ukrainian authorities stabilize the financial sector and implement reforms. Treasury advisors are already working closely with the Finance Ministry and National Bank of Ukraine, helping to develop strategies to manage existing liabilities, resolve failed banks, improve banking supervision, and spur financial intermediation. As Ukraine's needs evolve, Treasury will be in a position to deploy additional advisors with expertise in areas such as budget and tax administration.

Conclusion

As the United States and our international partners continue to confront Russia's illegal actions in Ukraine, we stand ready to further employ our arsenal of financial measures as the situation escalates. A diplomatic resolution to the crisis remains our goal, but if Russia choses to continue its illegal and destabilizing actions in Ukraine, we can impose substantial costs on, and expand the isolation of, an already weak Russian economy.

Thank you for the opportunity to testify in front of this committee. I am happy to answer your questions.

Chairman ROYCE. Thank you, Mr. Glaser.

From our standpoint and I think—I think it is pretty clear to the members here that our goal is to get a resolution to this thing as quickly as possible, to get some measure of reconciliation.

The Presidential candidates that are running on May 25th, they are mature candidates. They are going to push for the use of both Ukrainian and Russian. If we can get to the May 25th election, I think you have got a chance there for a huge turnout.

When we were in Dnipropetrovsk, when we were meeting with these Russian-speaking associations, representatives of women's groups, representatives of the Jewish community, and other minority communities, the uniform position, especially the different NGO groups, was that they were manning these ballot box stations to make certain that there was security for those who go to the polls.

Now, if you get the kind of turnout that at least we see in polling as anticipated, and you have this Presidential election followed by the election of local representatives from every district, I think we are on our way, potentially, to a system where we can begin to de-escalate this.

We have one big problem for the attempt by journalists to cover this story in the east and that is the disappearance of these journalists. We have got several journalists who have been disappeared by Russian separatists, taking them into custody. The campaign of intimidation, of course, is intended to shutter all indigenous outlets for uncensored news and information.

You have already got the seizure of the local broadcasting systems. So it suddenly becomes very, very important to support journalists going in to cover this election and also to counter Russian propaganda and that takes me to an issue I wanted to talk to Ambassador Nuland about.

The propaganda that you hear coming out of that part of the world is really in overdrive. Our committee recently passed legislation that is now signed into law, directing U.S. international broadcasts to be ramped up.

We are working on legislation to revamp and cut the bureaucracy over the top of Radio Free Europe and other surrogate broadcasters so that they can do the type of job they have done in the past.

And I was going to ask you, Ambassador, how do you assess our efforts in this information battle? How important do you think this is in terms of being able to get a flow of information into eastern Ukraine especially, so that people have the coverage going up to the election?

Because I think once the election occurs—and the other thing I will ask you to comment on: President Putin said in reference to the May election as you—as you quoted him—that he does not want to go forward with a referendum on the 11th. That is very good news, okay. But he also said he thinks the Presidential election on May 25th is a step in the right direction.

If we can build on this statement to get a huge turnout I think it increases the leverage for those in the country, in the east and the west, who want to see a reconciliation.

Ms. NULAND. Well, thank you, Mr. Chairman. We couldn't agree with you more that what is most important if you want to hear what the people of Ukraine have to say about their future is to let them vote. Let them vote across the country and most especially in the east and south of Ukraine.

I can talk at some length about how the OSCE assesses the electoral environment, which is surprisingly good with the exception of Crimea, of course, where people will have to be offered a place outside Crimea to vote and the Ukrainians are working on that, and a few of the most dangerous parts of Donetsk, including Slovyansk.

But the Ukrainians—in fact, Secretary Kerry spoke this morning to Prime Minister Yatsenyuk just before I came over here and one of the things that the Ukrainians are very focused on now is a "get out the vote" campaign across the country.

That speaks to the second part of your question, which is about free media. Would that Russia allowed it, would that the separatists allowed it, this would be the freest media environment Ukraine has ever enjoyed for an election.

But as you know, it is precisely that free media environment that is threatening to this illegally-armed movement and that is why some of the sites of occupation have included TV towers in Donetsk, Oblast, and in Luhansk.

The government has made a good effort to try to reclaim some of those, but when separatists seize TV towers they close out a plurality of voices and the Russian propaganda megaphone is the only thing that can be heard.

So we are very grateful to this committee. We are very grateful to the Congress for the support that you are showing for the programming we are helping the Ukrainians support.

We recently increased by $1.5 million our support to Ukrainian Government efforts to help prepare for the election and get truth out across. We are also, as you know, running and working on a very intensive effort with our allies and partners to support those voices trying to correct Russia's false narratives.

I think you have probably seen our United for Ukraine campaign, which is now only 5 percent government content. The other 95 percent is taken up by global supporters of Ukraine.

So these efforts are very important, but we are going to have to do more if this—if we are now back to the future and in a propaganda environment where truth is not an obstacle.

Chairman ROYCE. You gave us some numbers on the number of election observers that were being fielded-out by NGO groups in the U.S. and there are several thousand coming from Europe.

Do you have any estimate of how many NGOs or how many volunteers, election observers we are going to have on the ground in eastern Ukraine in order to try to monitor? And in southern Ukraine?

Ms. NULAND. I don't yet have a breakdown from the OSCE on their monitor posture, but I think it will be distributed across the country with 1,000 OSCE across the country. We would expect at least 500 of those in the south and the east. But that is the OSCE alone.

As I said, we are supporting some 3,300 indigenous Ukrainian NGO observers and they will be spread across the country, and that is before you get to what IRI, NDI and like institutions across Europe and from other countries will send.

So as I said, we expect this to be the best observed election in the transatlantic space since the end of the Cold War, per capita.

Chairman ROYCE. Thank you, Ambassador Nuland. My time has expired. We will go to Mr. Engel.

Mr. ENGEL. Thank you, Mr. Chairman, and once again thanks to both of you for the very, very fine work that you both are doing.

The equation for NATO since the fall of the Soviet Union has essentially been looking at Russia as a—as a partner, at least some kind of a partner. If this is no longer the case and Russia is now an adversary, not a partner, it changes the whole equation.

When we speak to the representatives of countries like Moldova, Georgia, Romania, Latvia, and Lithuania, they are all scared to death, and Russia has been pressuring them and we can only expect this pressure to increase in the coming months, particularly in Moldova and Georgia.

So what are we doing to support the rights of the people in these states in the region to choose their own futures and build democratic states? Because I really believe that if we don't step up to the plate on this you can almost kiss NATO goodbye because if we are not going to back up what we say we stand for then I think Putin will have won.

So I just think it is absolutely imperative that we reassure the other countries in the surrounding region who all come to see all of us and tell us that they have terrible fears of being collateral damage in this whole process.

Ms. NULAND. Thank you, Mr. Ranking Member. First, as I said, with regard to those countries who are members of the alliance, from the Baltic all the way down to the Black Sea, NATO is scoping and already deploying a massive reassurance mission on land, air, and sea.

I gave some details of that in my opening statement. We expect that mission to continue through the end of 2014 and we expect heads of state and government when they meet in Wales to review whether it needs to continue beyond that.

So Article 5—the traditional Article 5 reassurance of NATO is now going to be at a co-equal pillar yet again at the summit. With regard to the states who are partners of NATO—Moldova, Georgia, Ukraine itself—as you know, we have greatly increased our economic, our energy support to countries like Moldova who are most vulnerable to Russian pressure.

I have been out there twice. Secretary Kerry has been out there. A number of Members of Congress have been out to support them. The Prime Minister of Moldova was received in the White House, including by President Obama.

We are working with them on first diversifying their market away from Russia. As you know, the EU has now granted visa-free status to Moldova.

We are working to help them to explain in advance the benefits of Europe, including to the people of Transnistria, and we have worked a lot on imports of Moldovan wine, on energy interconnectors between Moldova and Romania to help them with reverse flow, et cetera, and reduce their energy dependence.

So those efforts will continue. In Georgia, as well, the new Prime Minister was here. We have had repeated visits including my own out there and those of Members of Congress and we are working with them primarily on strengthening rule of law, helping them prepare for their association agreement and to really maximize the trade and people-to-people benefits of their association with Europe.

Mr. ENGEL. Thank you. I want to ask you also a question about foreign assistance because in recent years it has diminished greatly for Central Europe and Eastern Europe.

There have been some improvements in some countries but in others needs have increased and at the same time, you know, the budget sequester, which I think was a disaster, there has been excessive budget cutting to these countries as a result.

So is the United States providing adequate assistance for Ukraine and other Eastern European countries now under Russian pressure and trying to consolidate their democracies? And if Congress provided more assistance would that help our efforts and what would be the effect on U.S. and regional security and what types of efforts might expanded assistance provide?

Ms. NULAND. Thank you, Congressman. As you know, as from your own efforts in Europe, once countries join the European Union they graduate from U.S. assistance. So at the current moment we don't provide much U.S. bilateral assistance. There are some programs that are active but very few for any of the countries that are currently in the European Union.

So our focus is to the east. It is certainly the case that in my budget, in the Bureau of European and Eurasian Affairs, we are shaking out the couch cushions and scraping the side of the pot to get more support of the kind I discussed for Ukraine in the first instance, but also for Moldova, for Georgia, for increasing U.S. trade opportunities for countries like Armenia that are feeling increasingly squeezed. With more we could, obviously, do more.

I want to just briefly mention another threat that I would like to have more resources to combat and that is the threat of corruption.

We see a new tool of outside influence, not just in the post-Soviet space, but increasingly in Central Europe and the Balkans, which is this corrupt oligarchical practices, dirty money flowing into these countries, buying politicians, then going into parliaments and dismantling democratic structures, dismantling free media, dismantling protections for NGOs.

I believe the United States has to do more to help countries across the European and Eurasian space resist this pernicious cancer of corruption, which is also a tool of outside influence and a threat to sovereignty for many of them.

Mr. ENGEL. Thank you. Thank you, Madame Chair.

Ms. ROS-LEHTINEN. Thank you very much, Ranking Member Engel.

The chair recognizes herself for 5 minutes.

The situation in Ukraine is indeed a powder keg ready to explode at any given moment. Putin is an unrepentant thug with an expansionist ideology who has thus far proven that he will not be deterred by the actions that the U.S. has taken in response to his aggressive moves in Ukraine and this is extremely dangerous for the stability of Ukraine and, indeed, the entire region.

His actions have been meant to destabilize Ukraine, foment pro-nationalist and anti-Western sentiments in Russia and manufacture a crisis so that he can play the role of the hero at home.

By creating this crisis, Putin is trying to mask the ills that he faces at home and who better to play his foil than us here in the United States?

With a growing number of Russians dissatisfied with the economy and his policies, the latest news that Putin is now supporting the May 25 election must be taken with a grain of salt because there are surely ulterior motives at play here.

I congratulate this committee under the leadership of Chairman Royce and Ranking Member Engel for the tough but fair bills that we have passed. Our President has issued several Executive orders imposing sanctions on Russian officials and that has gained some support in the EU. But I wanted to focus on the EU part.

We have been unable to get the EU on board for stronger, more effective sanctions. And so following up on your testimony, what more do we need to do to get the EU on board to impose additional sanctions? What are the major concerns and obstacles in getting the EU's backing?

And we had talked about Under Secretary Cohen's trip. What specifically will he—will the Secretary be pushing in his trip to Germany, France, and the U.K.? And there clearly has to be a U.S. strategy for dealing with Russia and a separate strategy toward Ukraine. But they must work together in order for us to be our most effective.

I believe that the administration is not willing to be strong enough in the face of Putin's aggression—doesn't wish to cause any more friction with Moscow. So we will then fall short of what is necessary to truly help the people of Ukraine who oppose Russian meddling over its sovereignty.

But perhaps the administration is unwilling to stand up to Putin's aggression because they are worried that we need his support for the chemical weapons program in Syria and our misguided negotiations with Iran over the nuclear program.

And if that is the case, then that just shows the consequences of our failed leadership, the fact that we are so desperate to keep a bad nuclear deal with Iran alive that we can't help those who are seeking our assistance because we don't want to upset Moscow too much.

Last month there were reports that our Department of Energy informed a Russian state-run nuclear corporation on suspension of cooperation projects. Can you provide us with an update on the status of our 123 Agreement with Russia and is there any discussion about reexamining our PNTR agreement with Moscow? So EU, Under Secretary Cohen's trip, and 123 and PNTR. Thank you.

Ms. NULAND. Thank you, Congresswoman. On 123 and PNTR, I am going to take the question. I, frankly, am not as briefed as I need to be.

With regard to the EU, why don't I start and then Assistant Secretary Glaser pick up? As you know, in the rounds of sanctions that we have had we have been able to move with the Europeans.

Their legislation, their legal base is somewhat different than ours. Their procedures are different. So it has been a matter of constant consultation with them to try to move in lockstep.

We have had success in the sanctions we have imposed for the occupation of Crimea on senior Russian officials responsible for orchestrating that and the violence in the south and east.

We are working now on encouraging the European Union to match the sanctions that the U.S. has put in place on those closest to Putin and their organizations because we do believe that those sanctions have had a serious impact on the Russian economy and, frankly, in destabilizing markets, which, as we both cited statistics, are the most impactful aspect.

And as I said in my testimony, what will have the biggest impact is if we move to sectoral sanctions. The President, as Assistant Secretary Glaser has made clear, has given us an Executive order that allows us to look at energy, banking, the defense sector, mining.

So we are now in intense consultations including those that David Cohen and Ambassador Dan Fried are engaged in this week on how those sectoral sanctions could work because they will be far——

Ms. Ros-Lehtinen. Well, thank you so much. As usual, I have talked too much and I ran out of time. So we will give you another opportunity. Maybe somebody will bring it up.

And so pleased to yield to Mr. Meeks of New York for his question and answer.

Mr. Meeks. Thank you, Madam Chair, Madam Secretary, Mr. Glaser. My line—my first questions were somewhat on the same line as Ms. Ileana Ros-Lehtinen but for different reasons.

I am always—I believe in sanctions when they are multilateral, not unilateral, you know, because unilateral sanctions don't seem to work. We don't—we are not able to really accomplish what our goal is when it is just us by ourselves and/or what effects they have on our allies who we work very closely with.

And so I want to make sure of that because I am very concerned about the aggression of Russia and I want to make sure that we do certain things but we are not isolating ourselves in the long run.

So it is important to me that we are in fact working with NATO and others in the Baltic States and every—because I know, for example, we met with some individuals from Latvia, for example, and they are saying it is important to have certain kinds of sanctions as opposed to others because it could be devastating to them and their country and cause turmoil within their own ranks and will end up hurting the very people that we want to help.

So with that being said, let me—let me ask this question. Do you feel that we are having the level of cooperation from our NATO allies, et cetera, as they understand the same vision? Are we on the same playing field with the vision of how we have got to fight back the aggression that has been moved—you know, as we see with Russia moving forward into the East Ukraine and Crimea?

Ms. Nuland. Thanks, Congressman. I would say that in the rounds of sanctions we have done heretofore we have moved largely in lockstep with Europe. There are some differences that have to do with the legal authorities and we are seeking to close the gaps that exist, as I said, and particularly with regard to those closest to Putin.

But as we get to sectoral sanctions it does get harder and the principles that you outlined are the same ones that we have. Assistant Secretary Glaser can speak to it. But we want to have more of an impact on the Russian economy than we have on our own.

We want to share the pain, if there is to be economic pain, across different sectors. That helps keep Europe together but it also ensures that one sector of our economy isn't hit harder than another.

We want to use a scalpel and not a—not a sledgehammer. We want to talk primarily about forward investment opportunities.

Mr. MEEKS. And as you have testified, of course, already having the door open because I am also a firm believer in diplomatic solutions. I don't think that anybody—I don't think really that a military solution, as some have hinted at, or giving of military equipment is the answer here.

I think that we have to try to figure out a way to do it through joint sanctions as well as with, you know, with our NATO allies, and then try to—hopefully that the Russians will end up coming to the diplomatic table and we can resolve this crisis on a diplomatic basis because—my next question would be—there are other serious issues that we still have to deal with Russia.

Last week, Principal Deputy Assistant Secretary of State Anita Friedt testified before this committee and I asked her about U.S.-Russian cooperation still because there were a lot of other things that we were doing with Russia.

And she informed me that despite the ongoing crisis in the Ukraine that the U.S. is still cooperating with Russia on certain matters such as nuclear arms agreements—that that's still going.

So I was wondering also, you know, in regards to Iran—dealing with Iran with the P5+1, could you tell us more specifically what is the status of our cooperation with Russia on other issues that are very important to us, for example, military cooperation and development and economic and anti-piracy and so on in dealing with Syria? Where are we with—are we still working in accord in those regards?

Ms. NULAND. Thank you, Congressman. We have, as you know, curtailed most of our bilateral economic work with Russia, most of our bilateral military-to-military.

But on all of the global issues that you mentioned, whether it is Iran, Syria, the arms control commitments that we have to each other, we have largely maintained these conversations. We don't do that as a favor to Russia.

Russia participates because it is in their interest to keep Iran from getting a nuclear weapon, et cetera. So those have largely continued.

Mr. MEEKS. And lastly—I have got 11 seconds, I don't know if I am going to get it in—I was wondering, do you think that the sanctions that are in place are affecting at all our cooperation with Russia?

Are they trying to push back saying, "Oh, if you don't stop these sanctions we are going to"—are they threatening us at all in that regard—threatening to stop cooperating on these international events?

Ms. NULAND. Again, heretofore the assessment holds that Russia cooperates in these issues not as a favor to us either, but because they judge them to be in their interest and that cooperation has continued.

Chairman ROYCE. Would the gentleman yield for 1 minute? One thing I did want to clarify and that is, Mr. Meeks, I have never heard anyone argue for a military solution. And as a matter of fact, in our conversations with the President of Ukraine and the Prime Minister of Ukraine, both made clear to us that they didn't expect any U.S. military involvement.

So I just did want to clarify that comment that you alluded to because I just, in the Senate or House, haven't seen any member——

Mr. MEEKS. I just heard several—some of our colleagues say that we should be giving some arms to the Ukraine or arming them in that regard and so that tells me——

Chairman ROYCE. That was the second half of your statement. But the first part went to a military solution. I just wanted to clear the record on that.

Let us go now to Mr. Chris Smith of New Jersey.

Mr. SMITH. Thank you so much, Mr. Chairman, and thank you to our two distinguished witnesses today for their work. I do have a couple of questions.

You know, the recent IRI poll suggested an overwhelming 84 percent of Ukrainian citizens said they will definitely or are likely to vote in the elections, including a substantial majority in the two regions in which the militants are very active. So that is a tremendous sign of ownership of their future.

And I do have a couple of questions. As co-chair of the Commission on Security and Cooperation in Europe, Ben Cardin and I will co-lead a delegation on the 25th of May to be election observers, and if any members here are interested please see me and, you know, perhaps you could join us in that effort.

But I do have some questions about the Ukrainian preparations for the elections, your thoughts on how well they are progressing, a breakdown of what voters-distant third.

But it did trigger a runoff. You know, we didn't get the winner. It was Yanukovych and it was judged to be a free and, you know, a true election with some discrepancy but largely free and fair.

The 2012 elections had more problems on the parliamentary level. So I am just wondering if enough safeguards are in place to ensure that this ballot even though there are 20 people running it probably is a two-way race between Poroshenko and Tymoshenko, although it may be a single winner because she is trailing significantly in the teens right now.

So I am just wondering if, you know, again, integrity of the ballot, people who vote, particularly in disputed areas, what precautions are being put into place to ensure their safety.

Ms. NULAND. Thanks, Congressman, and we are enormously grateful that you are going to lead an election observer team with Senator Cardin and we encourage anybody who has an interest to go because the more observers the better an election we will have.

First of all, just on what ODIHR, OSCE—ODIHR's findings are as of the middle of April—the Central Election Commission has met all of its legal deadlines, that it has registered 23 candidates, that there is a sound framework for free media, that there are 35.9 million registered voters—they have all registered online—that election commissions have been formed in virtually every one of the 225 districts.

There are 32,000 Presidential precinct election commissions. All of them, with the exception of those in Crimea and some locations in Donetsk, notably Slovyansk, are fully on schedule to prepare for these elections, including with regard to preparation of lists and all of those things.

Obviously, security leading up to the elections and on election day at polling places for election materials, et cetera, will be paramount. As I said, Secretary Kerry spoke to Prime Minister Yatsenyuk this morning.

The prime minster made clear that they are focused like a laser on this as they are on getting out the vote. They are also talking about—I think they are working with the OSCE now on alternative sites for Crimeans to exercise their right to vote if they choose and for places like Slovyansk where it may be too violent to vote.

But just to underscore where you started, the polling is indicating almost 70 percent of folks in the east of Ukraine are excited about casting their ballot, and that is the most—the best guarantee of political stability in Ukraine.

Mr. SMITH. Thank you. I appreciate that. Assistant Secretary Glaser, can you describe in more detail the sanctions that have been taken by our European allies? How effective do you think they have been in light of their financial, economic integration with Russia, particularly in the area of the energy sector?

Mr. GLASER. Yes, sure. I would be happy to try to answer that question. The European Union so far has focused its targeting on specific individuals that have been involved with the violation of the sovereignty of Ukraine and the incursion into Crimea.

That, in combination—I think it is—I think you can't really break out the impact of the European measures from the impact of the U.S. measures. I think you have to look at the situation in total and when you look at the—at the situation in total, again, Chairman Royce and I both rattled off some numbers as to what the impact has been to date in terms of impact on the Russian economy.

I think equally as important as that, although not quite as quantifiable as that, has been the market uncertainty that it creates—the chilling effect on further business dealings with Russia, on further investments in Russia. And what that does is it sets a framework—it sort of sets the table for us all to collectively take more significant action.

When Chancellor Merkel was here in Washington last week, she and President Obama made clear, as has Ambassador Nuland just now, that the next step in that would very likely be sanctions that target entities within sectors of the Russian economy. But there has been a lot of discussion about the financial sector or the energy sector, things like that.

That is precisely, and this gets to a question that was asked earlier, precisely what Under Secretary Cohen and Ambassador Fried are in Europe and in London, Paris, Berlin this week talking about because I do think that the U.S., even acting on our own, can exact costs on Russia.

I think we have demonstrated that. But, certainly, given the economic, financial, energy integration between Russia and Europe, anything that we do is going to be so much more effective in a multilateral context, both from an actual financial economic point of view and certainly from a political messaging point of view.

And what they are doing right now is sitting down with our European counterparts and going through, you know, concepts on how do we do this—how do we and Europe work together to have a very effective targeted set of actions against sectors of the Russian economy that, as Ambassador Nuland articulated, maximize the impact to Russia—on Russia while minimizing the impact on our own businesses and our own economies.

We understand that there are going to be costs to these actions. We understand that. But if we do it in a smart strategic way, we think we could have the impact that we are looking for and I am quite certain the that the Russians understand that very well.

Mr. SMITH. Thank you both.

Chairman ROYCE. Mr. Albio Sires of New Jersey.

Mr. SIRES. Thank you, Mr. Chairman, and thank you for being here. You know, along the same line as my colleague from New Jersey, these sanctions—I would think that in order for them to really be effective, the people of Russia have to feel it.

Do we have any evidence that the actual people, not just Putin's friends or the people in leadership, are impacted but this but the actual Russian people? Because it seems that his numbers keep going up as more popular and more popular as he makes these moves.

Mr. GLASER. Yes. I mean, it certainly sometimes takes time for damage to an economy to reflect in opinion polls with respect to leadership. But it is certainly the case that Russia is feeling on a very, very broad level the impact of the measures we have taken.

As we said, as recently as February, the IMF was forecasting a 2-percent growth for Russia. That is for Russia. That is not for Putin's inner circle. That is for Russia, and now it is forecasting near 0 percent and speculating that it might, in fact, be a recession. That is a recession for Russia as a whole.

So I think that the Russian leadership has to understand that the health of the Russian economy is very much at stake with respect to the measures we have taken and these are the initial measures that we have taken.

As we have said, we are in very, very intense consultations and discussions with Europeans on taking measures that would have an even greater impact on the Russian economy.

And as I said, I think that, even in and of itself, has created a level of market uncertainty that is continuing to damage the Russian economy quite broadly.

Mr. SIRES. Because it seems to me that these sanctions are directed at his friends, not necessarily the people of Russia. Is that accurate? I mean the people are the ones that are going to speak and say, ''Hey, let us stop this.''

Ms. NULAND. We have—as you know, sanction not only people in leadership, but also those close to Putin but what——

Mr. SIRES. Right.

Ms. NULAND [continuing]. But the effect has been general market uncertainty, which is affecting the whole economy.

For example, the cost of borrowing inside Russia is going up and up and up. Inflation is going up and up and up. I was in Europe last week talking to——

Mr. SIRES. Well, these are—these are what people are feeling.

Ms. NULAND. That people will begin to feel it. I was about to say that I was talking to a number of European business folks on a trip I took around allied capitals last week, including on sanctions, and business folks were reporting that Europeans are not making new investments, that the cost of their products exported to Russia are going up because of inflation, that they are not getting the orders for luxury goods because Russians are biding their time and waiting to see what happens.

So there is a lot of impact already. But our goal is not to hurt the Russian people per se. Our goal is to get Putin to change course.

Mr. SIRES. Well, you know, obviously, our goal is not to hurt the Russian people, but the Russian people are the ones that are going to speak to make sure that the leadership changes the course that they have taken.

Can you talk to me a little bit about this Russian colonial federalization, that they want the proposed amendment to the Constitution? What is this federalization? What does it mean? What are they talking about?

Ms. NULAND. Well, obviously, if I was still at the spokesperson's podium I would refer you to Russia as to what they are talking about.

But the original concept appeared to be such a broad decentralization of power that regions would have the right to independently vote to secede, attach themselves to Russia, et cetera, which, obviously, under nobody's Constitution, is the right way to go.

What the Ukrainian Government and what the Constitutional Reform Commission are offering, however, is very, very broad decentralization of authority and budgeting to local regions. Ukraine has been too centralized a state and that has been part of the problem.

But when Prime Minister Yatsenyuk was here, he gave a speech at the Atlantic Council in which he talked about devolving authority for everything except defense, foreign affairs, and some judicial functions to the regions—keep their own tax money, administer it themselves, education, language as well as electing their own officials.

So there is a really heavily decentralized future for Ukraine, but it needs to be achieved politically and not at the barrel of a gun.

Mr. SIRES. Thank you very much.

Chairman ROYCE. We go now to Mr. Dana Rohrabacher of California.

Mr. ROHRABACHER. Thank you very much, Mr. Chairman.

Ambassador Nuland, so what is the bottom line for the cost of all of this to the United States?

Ms. NULAND. As I—I gave some numbers, I believe, in my opening——

Mr. ROHRABACHER. Yes, you did.

Ms. NULAND [continuing]. With regard to Fiscal Year '13 and '14, so we are at $187 million, which is about where we have been in support for Ukraine over the last 5 years.

We have increased it by another $50 million in the loan guarantee.

Mr. ROHRABACHER. Well, that is just one program. But with all of the election observers—that includes the election observers and every——

Ms. NULAND. That includes the U.S. participation in the OSCE election observers.

Mr. ROHRABACHER. So it was $187 million?

Ms. NULAND. $187 million plus $50 million——

Mr. ROHRABACHER. Plus $50 million.

Ms. NULAND [continuing]. Which was appropriated on April 1st.

Mr. ROHRABACHER. Okay.

Ms. NULAND. $18 million from the Defense Budget for support for security services and border guards. But it is not that much more with the exception of the $50 million than what we have been spending in Ukraine over the years.

Mr. ROHRABACHER. Okay. Have we signed on into something with World Bank guaranteeing any loans, for example?

Ms. NULAND. So the—as you know, you have appropriated the—you have authorized the $1 billion loan guarantee, which scores at $400 million for the Treasury. With regard to the World Bank, they are just at the beginning of what they might be able to do to support. So I am not aware of any new loans that they have executed. I think they are going to wait and see how the elections go.

Mr. ROHRABACHER. Okay. So we are—we have spent about $200 million and we have got $400 million that we have scored for the guaranteeing of that loan.

Ms. NULAND. Which will come back to the U.S. Treasury when the loan is paid back, as you know.

Mr. ROHRABACHER. Right. When the loan is paid back.

Ms. NULAND. With interest.

Mr. ROHRABACHER. Right. Shall we all hold our breath for that? So do we have preferential payback then? Does that mean that all the other bills that the Ukrainian Government owes, they are going to have to pay us that $400 million first?

Ms. NULAND. Congressman, we will have to get you the details on exactly what the terms of this are.

Mr. ROHRABACHER. Yes. Okay.

Ms. NULAND. I think it is with the Treasury to do that.

Mr. ROHRABACHER. I think that that—we know what the answer to that is, but I would be happy to get it officially. Let me ask you this. When we were talking about the election—the best observed election—Yanukovych, of course, was the one who was elected the last time—a very well observed election, I might add.

Matter of fact, Chris Smith was there observing that election and gave that election a very big plus. Yanukovych was elected so he does represent a significant point of view in that country.

Is there someone from his party who is going to be on the ballot?

Ms. NULAND. In fact, his party, the Party of Regions, is fielding four of the 23 candidates who are registered. Communists are also there. Every single color of the political spectrum in Ukraine and every region is represented among the 23 candidates. So there is somebody for everybody to vote for.

Mr. ROHRABACHER. So it is better—it is more than just the best observed election. It is a legitimate election.

Ms. NULAND. That is what the OSCE assesses.

Mr. ROHRABACHER. Right. Well, we did have an election. We did have a legitimate election before and the elected President was removed after we had major street violence and reaction to his decision of going with an economic agreement with Russia rather than the EU.

About that street violence that happened that led to this—Mr. Yanukovych's removal, there were pictures that people—people were running around with these—that were, we were told, were neo-Nazis. Is that—were there neo-Nazis in those effort—street violence that led to Mr. Yanukovych's removal?

Ms. NULAND. First of all, the vast majority of those who participated on the Maidan were peaceful protestors. If you had a chance to see the pictures—many of us visited, including many members here—there were mothers and grandmothers and veterans and every——

Mr. ROHRABACHER. Yes. Let me note that I have——

Ms. NULAND. However——

Mr. ROHRABACHER. Before you go on, I saw those pictures as well. I also saw a lot of pictures of people throwing fire bombs at groups of policemen who were huddled in the—over in a corner.

There were people shooting into the ranks of police. So yes, there were mothers with flowers, but there were also very dangerous street fighters who were engaged in those demonstrations. The question is were there neo-Nazi groups involved in that?

Ms. NULAND. There were—as I said, almost every color of Ukraine was represented including some—including some ugly colors.

Mr. ROHRABACHER. So the answer is—the answer is yes then.

Ms. NULAND. But if I could say that with regard to the violence, all of those incidents are subject to investigation, notably including the deadly sniper incident in February, and there is good evidence to believe that there were outside agitators involved in that.

Mr. ROHRABACHER. Was there any indication that there were guns being involved with the anti-government demonstrators at that time?

Ms. NULAND. There is no question that as the protests became more and more virulent, and as the response of Yanukovych's police became more and more brutal, the tensions and the potential for use of weapons escalated on both sides——

Mr. ROHRABACHER. On both sides.

Ms. NULAND [continuing]. Which was why we were——

Mr. ROHRABACHER. That is correct.

Ms. NULAND [continuing]. So intent on a political settlement in February.

Mr. ROHRABACHER. I have one last question before my time is totally up and that is were those—the neo-Nazi groups that we are talking about here, which, again, were not dominating this.

There were very many, very good people, like you say, out demonstrating against this deal with Russia. They wanted to go with more of a European country than a pro-Russian country.

But those people who were not the good guys, but were part of that effort to push that country in that direction, were any of those neo-Nazi groups affiliated with any other Nazi groups in other countries?

Ms. NULAND. Congressman, what I can tell you—I don't know what the answer to that specific question with regard to the early period is.

What I can tell you is that in the violence and separatism that we have seen in the recent months, we have also seen recruiting on the neo-Nazi and fascist sites in Russia for volunteers to go participate in the seizing of buildings in Eastern Ukraine and the Ukrainians report stopping very large numbers of such people at the Ukrainian-Russian borders.

Mr. ROHRABACHER. I am sure. But you haven't seen that—any evidence that there are people in Western Europe—neo-Nazi groups that were supporting their brothers in Ukraine?

Ms. NULAND. I don't have any information to corroborate that. But I would refer you to the Ukrainians as they investigate these incidents of violence.

Mr. ROHRABACHER. Thank you.

Chairman ROYCE. Brad, did you want to yield for the moment? Okay. We go now to Mr. Ted Deutch of Florida.

Mr. DEUTCH. Thank you. Thank you, Mr. Chairman, and thank you, Mr. Sherman, for yielding.

I want to thank you, Mr. Chairman, and Ranking Member Engel for your continued focus on the crisis in Ukraine. You have acted swiftly and with resolve since Russia's first provocations and because of that the world knows where this Congress stands.

Ambassador Nuland, Assistant Secretary Glaser, as you are well familiar there are many moving parts to this situation. Rightfully, the United States has been in the forefront taking aggressive economic action to dissuade the Russian Government from any further meddling in the domestic events of another country, providing Ukraine with a loan guarantee and non-lethal military aid to bolster their ability to withstand subversive external pressure.

And we are working closely with our European allies to create a unified front against Russian influence in Ukraine. We must sustain this pressure until we are sufficiently reassured and can verify that the Russian Government will not continue to stir dissent within Ukraine's borders or threaten the territorial integrity of any of its neighbors.

But I want to talk about the way we are working with our European allies to achieve that. Ambassador Nuland, you had said earlier that sector-based sanctions may be something we consider if needed.

Now, for all of us who have been so involved in Iran's sanctions, it is the sector-based sanctions that we know are so effective and what I would like you to do is explain, one, what those sector-based sanctions will look like and, two, given that European trade with Russia is 10 times greater than that between the United States and Russia, what do we do to bring our European allies firmly on board, especially at a time when there are some in Europe—some former government officials who were deeply involved in the Russian economy?

What do we do? What should that look like? When will it be necessary and how do we ensure that we can go forward together with our European allies?

Ms. NULAND. Thanks, Congressman, and I would invite Assistant Secretary Glaser, who is the sanctions expert, to jump in here. But as we develop this sectoral approach, the idea here is, as I said, to use a scalpel rather than a hammer, to focus primarily on high-tech and other investment where Russia needs us far more than we need Russia.

I don't want to get into too much detail, but to say that the approach would also involve taking a sectoral slice across a bunch of different sectors at the same time such that the pain is shared among sectors of the economy and to help keep Europeans together because different ones are vulnerable in different sectors.

But we do think that we can be quite effective. I would note that whereas Europe trades 9 percent with Russia, Russia's trade is 50 percent based in Europe.

So they are far more vulnerable and we do believe that they are particularly vulnerable in the area of the high-tech imports that they need to take their economy to the next stage. I don't know if Assistant Secretary Glaser wants to add.

Mr. DEUTCH. Mr. Glaser.

Mr. GLASER. Thank you, Congressman, and thank you—thank you for the question. You know, you and I have spoken many, many times about strategically applying targeted sanctions. So I don't think I am telling you anything that you don't already know.

If you look at the way we have applied targeted measures in the past in a strategic way—it has been pursuant to an escalation, which, as you say in certain cases, culminated in broad targeting of sectors.

When that happened in the case of Iran, it happened well into the escalation and into the strategy and then it also happened, if you will recall, in that same summer in the context of Europe taking significant action to target virtually every bank that the United States was targeting and that is—all that together is why it was so effective.

Now, in this case, I understand that we are operating on a much more compressed time frame. There is much more urgency with respect to acting quickly on that and that is why you see us taking similar sorts of measures on a somewhat sort of compressed time frame.

We have started off by targeting individuals. We have targeted individuals, which have significant holdings throughout their Russian financial economic sector. I think we have already significantly weakened it and now we are in conversations with our European colleagues on how to, in a very smart way, do exactly what you want us to do, which is target sectors more broadly.

Mr. DEUTCH. I appreciate that. Just in my final seconds, I wanted to follow up on something that was in the New York Times on Monday. At the end of a report it said that Ukrainian security forces stopped the transport of contraband uranium that originated in Transnistria.

It is alarming that any amount of radioactive material would be in the hands of non-state actors, both for Ukraine's defenses and for regional security and stability. Can you comment on that report? We have not seen it widely reported. How concerned should we be? Where does this come from?

Ms. NULAND. Well, it just—it speaks to the lawlessness on borders and the fact that we are going to have to continue to help the Ukrainians going forward with border security. We are involved in supporting them in this incident.

Mr. DEUTCH. Right. Thank you, and thank you. I will yield back to the chairman. Thank you again, Mr. Sherman. But I—but I yield to Mr. Chabot.

Mr. CHABOT. Thank you. I appreciate the chairman yielding.

Madam Ambassador, let me start out with, first of all, relative to Crimea, there seems to be often in the stories that we read and the attitude and the statements that are made relative to Crimea that it is more or less a fait accompli now.

It has occurred. Russia won. It has now been annexed. Crimea is now part of Russia, which I certainly don't share that attitude, and I would like to hear what the administration has to say about that.

It is almost like we are completely focused now on, you know, Eastern Ukraine and we have to make sure that Putin doesn't do the same thing there he did in Crimea, but Crimea is gone, and I am very concerned about that attitude. Could you address that, please?

Ms. NULAND. We are concerned, too, Congressman. That is why in the most recent round of sanctions that we did, not the round a week ago but 2 weeks ago, we deepened and broadened the sanctions on those who have taken up illegal posts in Crimea.

We sanctioned all of the leaders of the illegal Crimean Government. We also sanctioned a major gas entity that had been expropriated by Russia and we are continuing to look at more targets in Crimea and more targets in Russia associated with Crimea and we will do that.

I would just take this opportunity to say that we are also gravely concerned about the deteriorating human rights situation inside Crimea where there appears to be a mirroring of some of the practices that Russia exercises at home.

Mr. CHABOT. Thank you. I would just urge the administration in both their statements and their interactions with Russia especially, but with our allies and everybody else not to fall into that trap where we just sort of, even without acknowledging that it is a fait accompli, and therefore let us move on and try to keep them from going even further because I do not think that we ought to consider Crimea to be an unalterable part of Russia at this point on.

Let me move on. In your statement, you had quoted President Obama, his March 20th statement, which I will quote again here: "America's support for our NATO allies is unwavering. We are bound together by our profound Article 5 commitment to defend one another," and that is our NATO allies.

Now, of course, Ukraine is not a member of NATO and so I just want to make sure here, is that unwavering commitment of our support or how wavering or unwavering is it for the Ukraine since they are not a part of NATO? Although the Clinton administration, of course, signed the Budapest Memorandum which, after Ukraine gave up their nukes basically—you can interpret it different ways but many would interpret it that the Brits and us and Russia more or less guaranteed or ensured the sovereignty of Ukraine, which has clearly been violated by Russia's actions here. Could you comment on just how unwavering our commitment to Ukraine is?

Ms. NULAND. Thanks, Congressman. The President's statement referred to our solemn treaty commitment ratified by the Senate to mutual defensive NATO allies. As you know, Ukraine is not a member of NATO and therefore is not covered by the U.S. security guarantee.

That said, we have had a long and deep 20-year security relationship with Ukraine and this Congress has authorized significant support for our military-to-military relationship, including helping Ukraine deploy with us to Afghanistan, to Kosovo.

We believe that some of the support we have given to the Ukrainian military over the years, including miliary education, contributed to their refusal to fire on their own people when Yanukovych wanted them to.

And then, as you know, in recent months, we have contributed $18 million in non-lethal assistance to Ukrainian security forces and to the border guards. As we mentioned, border guard—border defense is absolutely essential to keep separatists and thugs out of Ukraine.

Mr. CHABOT. Thank you. I have only got about 30 seconds left so I will be real quick on this final question. What is the administration and our allies doing to counter the Russian propaganda in the Ukraine and what is being done by the West and by the U.S., in particular, to assist Ukraine in disbursing the truth out there, particularly prior to an election?

We, obviously, don't want to get involved in who wins but what are we doing to get the truth out there?

Ms. NULAND. We have a very sizeable public diplomacy program in Ukraine. We also have mounted in the last couple of months, under Under Secretary for Public Diplomacy Rick Stengel's authority, an all-of-government effort to counteract Putin's lies. It includes our ''United for Ukraine'' Twitter campaign, which now has totally outstripped government.

Only 5 percent of the content is government. It is 95 percent now a public conversation. We put out a regular product twice a week to all of our Embassies, to all of our contacts in the media around the world and particularly in Europe, counteracting falsehoods and putting out truths.

We have recently increased the support we give to the Ukrainian Government for its own media center. But as we talked about at the beginning of the hearing, among the difficulties we face is this massive Russian propaganda campaign that includes separatists dismantling TV towers in the east of Ukraine to ensure that only Russian programming gets through. But also that there are no journalistic standards, including the standard of truth in what is being pumped out.

So it is very important and we are very grateful that you are continuing to look at how to get us back to the kinds of tools that we used to have for this kind of—this kind of an effort.

Mr. CHABOT. Thank you. Yield back.

Mr. ROHRABACHER. Yes. Mr. Brad Sherman.

Mr. SHERMAN. One of the thorniest issues in foreign policy is self-determination versus territorial integrity. We supported the independence of South Sudan and accepted the independence of Eritrea.

In Europe, we supported the independence of each of the republics of the Union of Soviet Socialist Republics. We supported the independence of each of the republics of the Federation of Yugoslavia. We created the independence of Kosovo.

On the other hand, we oppose the independence of Northern Kosovo. We oppose the independence of the Krajina region of Croatia, which was inhabited by Serbs. We oppose the independence of Abkhazia in South Ossetia and we, of course, oppose the independence or any other action with Crimea.

Seems kind of haphazard. In Moscow, they note, that although I have identified, like, 30 different decisions we have had to make in Europe that seem haphazard every single one of those decisions is the anti-Moscow decision.

What are our policies? When are we in favor of territorial integrity? When are we in favor of self-determination? When are we cheering on the people of South Sudan or Croatia? When are we opposed—why do we oppose the independence of Northern Kosovo? Is there—is it haphazard, Ambassador?

Ms. NULAND. Congressman, thanks for the opportunity to remind, that in keeping with the U.N. Charter, the United States and our European allies and most civilized nations on the planet oppose the changing of borders by force, and that is what happened in Crimea or that was the effort in Crimea. With regard to Kosovo——

Mr. SHERMAN. Are you saying that Northern Kosovo is not—well, that Kosovo was in force, South Sudan was in force?

Ms. NULAND. Kosovo was, first and foremost, a victim of a marauding military operation of ethnic cleansing by Milosevic, which, as you know, the international community spent more than a decade trying to pacify——

Mr. SHERMAN. Well, there was certainly force in the——

Ms. NULAND [continuing]. And the decision on independence was the result of a referendum of the people.

Mr. SHERMAN. The independence of several of the Yugoslav republics was achieved by force. There are—it is not like every time we have supported independence it was some clean, bloodless operation.

But I will agree with you the people of Kosovo had—survived some terrible onslaughts that caused for change. Let me shift to another issue. Has the Right Sector militia been disarmed and has Kiev tried very hard to disarm them?

Ms. NULAND. The Government of Ukraine has made a massive effort to disarm the Pravy Sector—to lock up those leaders who have been found to use violence. They are also putting them on trial. They have also offered a weapons buy-back program and they are working very intensively in the——

Mr. SHERMAN. How successful has that effort been?

Ms. NULAND. They have made significant progress and there is more progress to make.

Mr. SHERMAN. The Language Law of 2012 in the Ukraine gave special treatment or security to those who speak Russian. There was an attempt to repeal that law. I believe that repeal was vetoed.

Has the——have the leaders of the Ukraine committed to their own people or committed to the world that they are willing to keep that law in force or are we in the United States in a situation where we may suffer costs and disruption and danger because Kiev wants to repeal a language law?

Ms. NULAND. Well, as you said, Congressman, that effort to repeal the law was vetoed by Acting President Turchynov. The Ukrainian Constitutional Commission and the current government have made broad statements to the effect that language rights will be protected in the constitutional reform process.

You know that Ukraine currently has one of the most liberal language regimes in the world where, if you have 10 percent local population they can study, they can have local services in their local language.

So the expectation is that that will be continued, but it is a matter for the Ukrainian people to decide——

Mr. SHERMAN. Let me——

Ms. NULAND [continuing]. In the constitutional reform process.

Mr. SHERMAN. Will you squeeze in one more question? Some have proposed that we export natural gas to the Ukraine. The Ukraines can't afford to buy that natural gas for $10 a unit from Russia.

The Japanese bid $15 or $16 per unit for natural gas that they purchase on the world market, which means anybody exporting natural gas from the United States would sell it to the——for the world market price.

Do you know of a pot of money that would allow us to subsidize Ukrainian natural gas purchases that came from us and from our private companies? Do you got tens of billions of dollars lying around to do that?

Ms. NULAND. Congressman, it is not——it is not actually going to go that way. What we are working on to help Ukraine with its energy independence are a number of things. The fastest short-term step is to help with reverse flows of gas from the European market into Ukraine.

We have worked intensively with the EU, with Slovakia, with Ukraine to get that reverse flow going. It is also coming now from Poland, from Hungary.

Mr. SHERMAN. And but——

Ms. NULAND. But over the longer term it goes to Ukraine's own resources——

Mr. SHERMAN. Ambassador, you have——here in Congress we are all talking about exporting U.S. gas to the Ukraine. So that was the question, but we will have to go on to someone else.

Mr. ROHRABACHER. Thank you very much. Next we have Judge Poe.

Mr. POE. I thank the chairman. Thank you for being here. I share my friend's frustration with U.S. foreign policy because even though I thought he asked the question very well about when do we support self-determination and when do we support a current government, sorry, I didn't get an answer.

I don't know what our policy is. It seems to me like a decision is made at the time and I am not sure whose interest it is made in.

It seems to me that the Russians—and I was in Ukraine with some other Members of Congress and saw first hand the people at Maidan and also saw the memorial to all that were killed by the old government—the civilians.

The Russians believe in creating a crisis in somebody else's country, unrest—political unrest—and then the Russians want to go in militarily or some other way and solve the unrest.

It seems like they did that in Georgia. The world got all upset about the Russians taking one-third of the Georgian country, but the Russian tanks are still there. I saw them not too long ago. And now they went into Crimea. The world said that is not nice and they are still there.

It looks to me like they are moving into the eastern part of Ukraine. I think we have a map, if we could show this—members also have their own personal copy, if we can put this map up, let me just know when you are ready—of what the Russian troops look like on the Ukrainian border.

It is a little scary if you live on that side of Ukraine, and I met with other countries—Moldova—in Parliament yesterday. They all want to talk about we are next—we think the Russians are taking us next, and other countries are very concerned that the Russian mode of operation is to cause a crisis, go in, solve the crisis, intimidate countries. And I think that is what they want to do with Ukraine—intimidate them into ceding some of that land.

But we shall see. Is the purpose of the sanctions—American sanctions—to stop the Russians where they are? Or is the purpose of the American sanctions to say you not only can't go any further, you have got to give Crimea back? Which of those two? It has got to be one or the other.

Ms. NULAND. The latter, Congressman.

Mr. POE. So we want them out of Crimea?

Ms. NULAND. We do not recognize their occupation of Crimea and they need to roll back, and they need to get their 40,000 troops off Ukraine's borders as well. I have talked, as you just did, about the arsonist setting the fire and then coming in dressed as the fire-man——

Mr. POE. Oh, yes.

Ms. NULAND [continuing]. And then occupying the building.

Mr. POE. And the Russian special forces going into Georgia dressed like Georgians, if you will, and then they come in to Crimea and now in Eastern Europe and they cause the hostilities. There are Russian special forces causing these disturbances, according to some reports. Do you believe those reports, Ambassador?

Ms. NULAND. We have high confidence, I can say, in a setting like this of Russian involvement in the planning, financing, and organizing of these efforts to destabilize Eastern Ukraine, including the presence of Russian agents.

Mr. POE. I would say that the purpose of sanctions—I don't think it worked, in all fairness. I don't think they stopped Russians from doing anything.

But if we impose further sanctions, I hope we are careful that we don't punish American companies. We punish—if we are punishing somebody, we punish the Russian economy, if you will, and are careful about what we do to American companies.

I think, you know, as far as the sanctions go I think, to coin a phrase, the proof is in the Putin and in this case it hasn't seemed to stop him at all in what he wants to do.

Here is a map. You have, I think, a small one there in front of you. I hope somebody gave you the small one. If you can't see it then we will come back to it before my 5 minutes is up. Supply the witnesses with a smaller map. It is not a trick question.

I just want you to look at it, see if you agree that this might be the Russian mode of operation and where the Russians are on Eastern Ukraine.

Georgia, I want to go back to Georgia—their security operation, they want to be in NATO. Does the United States—on the upcoming NATO conference—do we support offering Georgia a MAP? We support that?

Ms. NULAND. We have long believed that Georgia has met the criteria for MAP. The concern is that we have to have 28 votes in the alliance in order to grant them MAP and we don't have them at the moment.

Mr. POE. Okay. I do believe we ought to help Europe economically, and it is one way we need to—we can help this crisis is if we give the Europeans—not just Ukraine but Europeans an alternative to Gazprom. I was in Ukraine when the Russians turned the gas off. It was cold. It was dark. They need an alternative.

We have got an abundance of both natural gas and crude oil. I would hope the administration would expedite the sale to Europe of those products to give competition to ease the tensions in the area.

I am almost out of time. If I could ask one more question, Mr. Chairman. Lok at the map that I just showed you. If I were Ukrainian I would be a little nervous about all the Russian movement from Russia up to the border.

Do you think that is a fair analysis of what the Russians have done toward Ukraine? Either one or both of you. That will be my last question.

Ms. NULAND. We do believe that this deployment of troops ringing Ukraine's border is designed to be intimidational, yes.

Mr. POE. And they are still there?

Ms. NULAND. They are. They have been on high alert for some 3 months. It must be extremely expensive.

Mr. POE. All right. Thank you both. I yield back, Mr. Chairman.

Chairman ROYCE. Thank you, sir. The chair will now recognize Mr. Keating from Massachusetts.

Mr. KEATING. Thank you, Mr. Chairman. You mentioned briefly about the human rights issues in Crimea and I am concerned particularly with the Tatar population that is there.

In response to peaceful protests, Russian authorities have reportedly beaten some Tatar leaders, forced others into exile. Russian authorities have also threatened to shut down Tatar communities' Parliament.

What is your assessment, particularly of the Tatar population in Crimea, and do you expect any tensions in that regard to even grow when we get around to May 18th and the 70th anniversary of the Soviet Union's forced deportation of Crimean Tatars?

Ms. NULAND. Congressman, we are extremely concerned about the human rights situation for all Crimeans, but notably for Tatars. I think you know what we know, which is, first and foremost, that the Crimean Tatar leader himself, Mustafa Dzhemilev, has been banned from Crimea until 2019.

We had a Euromaidan Crimean activist abducted in Sevastopol and tortured. We have had more than 7,000 IDPs come out of— come out of Crimea in this period.

The local Crimeans are being told that they have to vacate their property, give up their land and, as you say, the 70th anniversary is coming. So our grave concern is that Russia is cloning its local human rights practices in Crimea now.

Mr. KEATING. There is one thing I think that is important to underscore to those from the outside looking at today's hearing and that is the fact that when we are talking about our actions and we are talking about diplomatic solutions, it is important to really underscore the fact that this isn't about Russia and the United States determining the future of Ukraine, but the Ukraines—the Ukrainian people themselves.

What can we do to continue to get that message across to the rest of the world? You made it clear, I think, here to us that that is important, but I think it is an important message to underscore.

Ms. NULAND. Absolutely, Congressman, and that speaks, first and foremost, to ensuring that this election on May 25th, where every eligible Ukrainian voter—north, south, east or west—gets a chance to express their will about their future from a slate of 23 candidates, takes place.

But it also speaks to the great care that we are taking in our diplomatic conversations with Europe, with Russia, with the OSCE. Nothing about Ukraine without Ukraine. They must be part of all of this.

Mr. KEATING. Great. An important point, and I yield back, Mr. Chairman.

Mr. CONNOLLY. Would the gentleman yield?

Mr. KEATING. Yes. The gentleman yields to——

Mr. CONNOLLY. I thank the gentleman, and welcome to both of you. Mr. Glaser, you particularly enumerated, as did Ambassador Nuland, the economic consequences to Russia, and they are growing. To what extent do we believe that Putin is feeling that pressure from his own business community and is cognizant of the macroeconomic consequences that can ensue, even absent sanctions just because of their behavior—his own behavior?

Ms. NULAND. Congressman, one of the parlor games that I have found it unlucky to play is to try to get inside the head of President Putin and speculate as to what he knows. But the facts and the economic statistics are—could only smack any sane person in the head. So——

Mr. CONNOLLY. Do you think he calculated that and made a calculated risk when he did what he did in Crimea nonetheless? I mean, you just said, "sane person." Certainly, you don't think Mr. Putin is something other than sane, do you?

Ms. NULAND. I didn't mean to make any calculation with regard to his mental state. But I do believe that——

Mr. CONNOLLY. Do you want to speculate?

Ms. NULAND. But I do believe that the degree to which the Russian economy is integrated now into the global economy, which is a different situation than the one that he grew up with, causes vulnerabilities that may not be well understood by folks who don't work in the business sector day in and day out.

Mr. CONNOLLY. Yes. And let me just ask one more question real quickly. I want to go back to the whole question of our European allies.

There have been some, both in the media and here in Congress, who kind of look at our State Department, our approach on possible sanctions—coordinated sanctions as a bit of a feckless enterprise, given the reluctance of the Europeans, frankly, to do anything tough, and perhaps we haven't been all that tough on them to get tough. I wonder if you would comment on that.

Mr. GLASER. I am happy to try to take that question, Congressman. I think that we have been quite tough to date and I think that things are only going to get tougher and tougher for the Russians if the situation continues to escalate. I think the President has made that quite clear.

Mr. CONNOLLY. Mr. Glaser, the question, though, was how tough are the Europeans willing to be and how tough are we being on them to be so?

Mr. GLASER. Well, I think last week President Obama and Chairman Merkel stood—Chancellor Merkel stood up together and made quite clear that if the May 25th elections were disrupted then the United States and Europe were going to take significant actions and President Obama made quite clear that very well could include sectoral sanctions.

And on the heels of that, we have a very senior group—Under Secretary Cohen, Ambassador Fried—in Europe right now working with the Europeans to determine exactly what that would be.

Europe works sometimes on different processes than we have. We have certain advantages in the way our sanctions program works. It allows us to be a bit faster and sometimes we are a bit stronger and I don't think we should be shy about that.

I think the key is that we are both moving in the same direction, creating the market uncertainties and I think we are doing that and I very much hope that when we—that if things don't go as we want them to go with respect to the elections, we are going to be prepared to take very, very significant measures that will have significant impacts on the Russian economy and that would include the Europeans as well.

Ms. NULAND. I would just add that in every single diplomatic conversation between any European and any American at any level over the last 6 weeks the issue of sanctions has been topics one, two and three along with our efforts to work with Europe to de-escalate the conflict.

Chairman ROYCE. We are going to go to Mr. Ron——

Mr. CONNOLLY. I thank my friend.

Chairman ROYCE [continuing]. DeSantis from Florida.

Mr. CONNOLLY. Yielding.

Mr. DESANTIS. Thank you, Mr. Chairman. Ambassador Nuland, does the administration assess that the actions of Russia may require us to relook at our force posture in Europe and our requirements for future deployments, exercises and training in the region?

Ms. NULAND. Congressman, I would say that the NATO reassurance mission that you are seeing begin to deploy out and which I spoke about at the beginning already constitutes a change in the way we are postured, that reassurance in Article 5 have come back to the forefront of the alliance's business.

With regard to the medium and the long-term, I think it depends on what we see from Russia and whether we are able to de-escalate this. As you know, the current mission, which has land, air and sea reassurance and visible exercising, goes through the end of 2014.

When we have our NATO summit in Wales in September, we will evaluate just the question that you have, whether more needs to be done and where and how.

Mr. DESANTIS. So at this time there is no either commitment or plan to have a presence on a more permanent basis in some of the region?

Ms. NULAND. I think that we are open to doing what is—what is necessary as we see the situation evolve. But I would simply say that it has already caused the Pentagon to look at plans that it had about how to posture globally and they are working on that now.

Mr. DESANTIS. And some of our allies—our NATO allies like Latvia, Estonia, Lithuania, Poland—what have they, if anything, asked of us in this regard?

Ms. NULAND. We have fulfilled—the U.S. has fulfilled all of the asks that we have had, which were primarily for increased air policing and for ground troops. As I said at the outset, we have 750 U.S. troops now, including deployments in all of the Baltic States, and that has been very reassuring.

They have also wanted the high-level visits that they have had from Members of Congress, from the Vice President, from others. We will continue to look at what more might be appropriate.

As you know, we opened a new base in Estonia or we supported use of an Estonian base for NATO missions. So we will keep looking at that.

Mr. DESANTIS. Now, in light of what has happened with Ukraine, Putin has taken this position that well, look, all these people are Russians—I am actually saving them by violating Ukrainian sovereignty, and that same argument could obviously be applied to Latvia, Estonia, and some of our NATO allies because they have ethnic Russian populations.

And so if that kind of pretext were used in some place like Latvia, you would—the administration's position would be that Article 5 of NATO would, clearly, be invoked?

Ms. NULAND. Absolutely. We have a solemn treaty commitment to our NATO allies.

Mr. DESANTIS. And how do you—and maybe this is just news reports, but there have been some reports coming out of Latvia of—even though we have assured them that we stand shoulder to shoulder, there is a lot of fear about what would happen and whether we would be willing, if push came to shove, to actually stand with them.

So I am wondering—is that something that you have received from folks in Latvia or is that kind of the press puffing this up?

Ms. NULAND. No. They are very concerned. They are now frontline states, a word I never wanted to use again in my career, but we have to use now. So that is why the physical reassurance of having American ground troops, having American planes in the air and now working with other allies to also join us in the Baltic states, in Poland, in Romania, in Bulgaria is so important.

Mr. DESANTIS. So, but is the fear—of course, there is fear from—about Russia may do, but is there—is that fear amplified because of perhaps not knowing what we may do or do you think that they are satisfied that we would be there to support them?

Ms. NULAND. Again, I think the reassurance mission and the arrival particularly of ground troops has gone a long way toward making it clear that we intend to honor our commitments. But we have to continue to talk to them and evaluate what they need.

Mr. DESANTIS. Thank you for that, and I yield back the balance of my time.

Chairman ROYCE. Thank you. We go now to Mr. David Cicilline of Rhode Island.

Mr. CICILLINE. Thank you, Mr. Chairman, and I thank you for this hearing and also for leading our delegation recently to Ukraine. I thank Ambassador Nuland and Secretary Glaser for being here.

I think it is very clear and I hope this hearing reinforces the notion that there are tremendous consequences, obviously, for the Ukrainian people for what is currently happening there, but also for the region and, ultimately, significant geopolitical consequences for the world, including the national security of our own country.

So we—I think we are—our assessment is the same as yours, that there was significant evidence of Russia's involvement in planning, organizing and inciting events inside of Ukraine and we were also, I think, struck by the overwhelming Ukrainian support for a unified democratic country and that includes in Crimea.

And I think, you know, to build on a question earlier about our ability to kind of support a response to this incredibly sophisticated, incredibly well-financed Russian propaganda machine that includes taking over television stations and denying access to Ukrainian television so they are receiving all of their information from Russian television.

And I was very happy to hear the efforts that you described and whatever else you think we can do in the Congress to support that.

I think it is critical. I know it is an important issue the chairman raised, but we saw lots of evidence of that.

Second thing I want to mention is there was a recent report in the Sunday New York Times that began to reveal some of the kind of wealth that President Putin has accumulated and questioned some of the ways in which that has happened, and it would be useful, I think, for the world to understand more about that.

And to the extent that the State Department and others can share that information I think the Russian people have a right to know that. Certainly, the Ukrainian people have a right to know that.

What I want to ask you about is specifically, Ambassador Nuland, is the NATO and European response. While your fourth pillar spoke about the importance of kind of reassuring our NATO allies and, obviously, that is critical, but I also hope it is an opportunity for our NATO partners to reexamine their own commitments to NATO and to sort of understand that they have maybe, in almost every instance but I think four countries, not met the requirements, and while this is of grave concern to us because of the geopolitical implications, it is on the front door of many of our European allies, and so I would like you to speak to that.

Do they understand that? Are they beginning to use this as an opportunity to kind of reawaken the importance of NATO and recommit to its role? And then, secondly, if you would just speak to the human rights violations in Crimea to the extent that you can. I think we should know as much about that as we can. And I want to also mention before I forget to thank you for your staff that were a part of accommodating our visit. It was a very productive visit and the Embassy staff there were outstanding.

Ms. NULAND. Thank you, Congressman. We are very proud of our Embassy in Kiev led by Ambassador Pyatt. First, with regard to the new reality that NATO cannot simply be an exporter of security beyond its space, as we had been focusing on throughout the past 20 years, but that Article 5 is back as an area of primary focus for the alliance, I think it has been a wake-up call for all of us and if, as you saw when the President was in Europe in March, and I think you will see when he goes back to Europe in June, he is availing himself of every opportunity he has with European leaders to say it is time now to reverse the slide in European defense spending.

He certainly raised that with Chancellor Merkel. He will raise it with everybody else, and we are looking for each ally to do their part going forward. And, frankly, this reassurance mission is not cheap either so people are having to find budget and find capability.

With regard to the human rights abuses in Crimea, I don't know if you were in the room when I answered Congressman Keating's question, but I went through some of what we are seeing—first and foremost, the Crimean leader himself being blocked from returning to Crimea until 2019, 7,200 IDPs, mostly Crimean Tatars, having fled from the Crimean Peninsula, concerns that local authorities have now announced the Crimean Tatars are going to have to vacate their property, give up their land, particularly if they refuse to take Russian citizenship.

So very, very concerned now that the human rights standards of Russia have migrated to Crimea.

Mr. CICILLINE. And just if I could ask one final question. I think the chairman mentioned this—from everyone that we spoke to, they all see the Presidential elections on May 25th as a very important turning point and all of the efforts of the Russians and particularly President Putin to destabilize Ukraine to try to prevent those elections from happening as a key strategy of the sort of aggressive—aggression plan.

Are there additional things we can be doing or encouraging our European partners to do to make sure those elections happen and that they are free and fair and that the Ukrainian people get to decide who their democratically elected President will be?

Ms. NULAND. Well, as we have been saying, you are absolutely right. This is the opportunity. If you really care what the people of the East think, let them vote and let them vote for one of these 23 candidates. Let them express themselves politically.

So this speaks to two pieces of the strategy. One is all the effort that we and the Europeans are putting into the strongest possible OSCE ODIHR monitoring mission in the transatlantic space ever and the $11 million the U.S. has given to help ensure free, fair elections and training.

The second piece is what we are talking about in terms of the President's press conference with Chancellor Merkel where he said efforts by Russia to destabilize or prevent these elections from happening will result in sectoral sanctions.

That is why we are working so hard now to prepare these sanctions so that that stick is visible and is real and is well understood, because we all have to let the Ukrainian people have their say.

Mr. CICILLINE. Great. Thank you. Thank you, Mr. Chairman. I yield back.

Chairman ROYCE. Thank you, Mr. Cicilline. We now go to Mr. Ted Yoho of Florida.

Mr. YOHO. Thank you, Mr. Chairman. Thank you both for being here. I want to touch on Crimea again because you were talking about it and it was one of my questions and you answered most of it. What is the atmosphere and environment of the pro-Russian people in Crimea?

You just answered about the human rights violations. What are you seeing over there? Are they—do they—are they on edge? Do you see the country stabilizing? It doesn't sound like it, and are they accepting the separation?

Ms. NULAND. You are talking about how do ethnic Russians in Crimea feel about what has happened?

Mr. YOHO. Yes, ma'am.

Ms. NULAND. I don't think it is a secret that they are not sad about what is happening, but there is a great amount of instability and lack of confidence in what comes next, including whether they are going to get the enormous investment that Russia has promised in their economy.

Mr. YOHO. All right. Are you seeing a functioning government there with the people they have elected?

Ms. NULAND. Frankly, I am not going to take that one because I haven't looked at it very carefully.

Mr. YOHO. Okay. I want to ask you both about the $1 billion loan guarantee that we voted here on, which I voted against, but I didn't get it recorded.

Have we given guaranteed loan guarantees to Ukraine before?

Ms. NULAND. It is conceivable that we did a facility similar to this in the '90s. I will have to—we will have to check.

Mr. YOHO. Okay. I am going to submit that and I would like an answer on that. And the reason I bring that up is after that vote we had, somebody came to visit our office and they thanked me for my vote and I told them I had voted against it and he goes, ''I know you did, but we realize that is a gift to the Ukrainian people that we will never pay back,'' and that kind of bothered me and I shared that with some other Congressmen and they said they had no idea of that.

So I want to check into that. If we are going to help out a country, I would like to get the money back, especially in these tough economic times.

You had also brought up working with Russia in Syria and the work that we have with them—you see that going forward with the destruction of the chemical weapons. Seems like we have done a pretty good job of getting most of those. Do you see that continuing and Russia working with us on that?

Ms. NULAND. Well, as you know, our cooperation with Russia on Syria has been mixed. But in the area of chemical weapons, we have largely worked fine together. We have now pulled, I think, 92 percent of the chemical weapons out. We have a final 8 percent.

Secretary Kerry, as you know, has had probably three phone calls with Foreign Minister Lavrov over the last 2 to 3 weeks to try to concert U.S. and Russian efforts together.

Mr. YOHO. Okay. I just want to make sure that was going that way and I hope that continues. And what about future space flights and returning our astronauts? Because that one person said that we could use a trampoline and, you know, those kind of working relationships—do you see those continuing?

Ms. NULAND. That aspect of our space relationship is expected to continue, yes.

Mr. YOHO. All right. And then——

Ms. NULAND. Because it benefits both Russia and the United States.

Mr. YOHO. Okay. And then you were talking about helping Ukraine secure its borders and the amount of money that we have given—I think you said $187 million, plus $50 million, plus another $18 million. And you said—had alluded that we had given them approximately $750 million over the last 5 years. You said roughly $180—$150 to $180 million a year.

Yet the reports I have read say that the Ukrainian Government was wrought with corruption. There were human rights abuses, and I even heard reports of human trafficking.

If they had a functioning government now, to go in there now, what is going to make the dynamics different that they are going to secure the border and do those things that we wish them to do with the money that we are lending them or giving them? Not lending, giving.

Ms. NULAND. Well, first of all——

Mr. YOHO. Hard-working American taxpayers' money.

Ms. NULAND. Right. The vast majority of money we have given to Ukraine over these years has not gone to the government. It has gone to support independent efforts and to support the NGO sector and to support Chernobyl and those kinds of thing.

But going forward, among the things that the transitional government has already gotten through is the first real anti-corruption legislation that we have seen in Ukraine through all of these years.

So as part of the IMF program preparation, they supported broad public procurement, transparency legislation, changes in the way energy is dealt with, the agricultural sector, a lot of these sectors that have been rife with corruption. Now, granted, these are setting a legislative bar and they now have to be implemented.

But it was precisely fighting corruption that was one of the main motivators for the Maidan movement in the first place. So the expectation is that there will have to be, whoever is elected, broad implementation now to clean up Ukraine.

Mr. YOHO. Thank you for your answers. I yield back.

Chairman ROYCE. Thank you, Mr. Yoho. We now go to Dr. Ami Bera of California.

Mr. BERA. Thank you, Mr. Chairman, and thank you, Ambassador Nuland and Mr. Glaser.

You touched on the propaganda machine that is coming out of Russia and Moscow and the control of media and information, which, if we look back at history, is critical and particularly history in this part of Eastern Europe.

Going back to World War II, going back to the Cold War, one mechanism to control the masses and one mechanism to get people fighting against each other was that propaganda machine and that control of the free flow of information.

I was glad to hear that we are helping the Ukrainian people use social media. The Twitter account was United Ukraine—the hashtag. So what are some other mechanisms that we are doing to help the Ukrainian people, empower them and get access to credible information?

Ms. NULAND. Well, as you mentioned a couple of them. So putting forward our own positive information, helping them to get information translated, not just in Ukrainian, but in Russian out to counteract all of this.

We are supporting the government's media center so that they can get positive decisions on decentralization and constitutional reform out in Russian, in Ukrainian, in English as quickly as possible.

We are also supporting independent media and particularly digital media because that is harder to take down. We support digital media in Russia and in Ukraine and that was very effective during the Maidan period in getting instant communications.

But as I said, at the beginning it is very difficult an environment where Russia is taking down the infrastructure.

Mr. BERA. Right, and so a lot of that infrastructure may not have existed in the first place, but in terms of cell phone capability and so forth and using hand-held devices, have they taken that infrastructure down as well?

Ms. NULAND. Well, it is primarily the TV capacity, which is where the vast majority of Eastern Ukrainians get their—get their news. So that has been the problem.

But the government, in its operations to liberate entities, has put a priority on liberating TV towers and they did get two back just in the last week. But, as you know, when truth is optional, it is difficult. So our truth and their truth is what we need to get out.

Mr. BERA. So we certainly, under Chairman Royce's leadership, you know, are very supportive of increasing our ability—you know, Radio Free Europe and other capabilities, to get information out and so forth.

The other thing that I find disturbing, you know, a month ago, you know, again, on this kind of propaganda and turning people against each other, I found the anti-Semitic fliers that were distributed incredibly reprehensible and very worrisome, given the history.

Some of the worst tragedies of the Holocaust occurred in Ukraine and to, you know, really look at some of these fliers and they very much are reminiscent. You know, asking members of a large and vibrant Ukrainian Jewish community to register or face deportation, you know, just rings of some trends that are worrisome.

I am glad that the administration and Secretary Kerry came out very strongly against these, and while we don't know where they came from, it is actions like that that I find worrisome.

Have we seen other trends against, you know, not just the Ukrainian Jewish population, but many folks in my community fled Russia, fled Ukraine in search of religious freedoms and settled in the Sacramento area. Are we seeing other forms of propaganda or hate?

Ms. NULAND. We are, not just in Crimea, against all minority communities. I can give you some things here. On April 22nd, the Holocaust Memorial in Sevastopol was sprayed with a red hammer and sickle. The Slovyansk TV tower that was taken over began broadcasting anti-Semitic programming.

We have had Roma fleeing particularly from Slovyansk, but other parts of Eastern Ukraine under threats of intimidation. There have been death threats against the chief rabbi of Crimea, who has now fled.

Pro-Russian thugs kidnapped priests of the Ukrainian Greek Catholic Church in Crimea, interrogated them. So it is bad. It is bad.

Mr. BERA. So just in the few remaining moments, given the history and some of the tragedy and atrocities that have taken place in Ukraine during the Holocaust, you know, we have to be very vigilant in standing with this and, you know, I think on behalf of this entire body we find those acts reprehensible and unacceptable.

Ms. NULAND. As do we.

Chairman ROYCE. We go now to Mr. Adam Kinzinger of Illinois.

Mr. KINZINGER. Thank you, Mr. Chairman, and thank you both for being here and for serving your country in such a capacity. I apologize I was not here for most of the hearing so I hope I don't touch on questions that were already asked.

I want to stress a very important thing that I think gets lost in this and that is my concern of this idea that we are not hearing much of a discussion about Crimea anymore and it is almost a feeling that Crimea is just going to go to Russia, and I understand the difficulties that we are dealing with and the nature of this whole situation.

But I would just remind everybody in the—about the situation in Ukraine that an agreement was signed by these countries to respect the territorial integrity of a country that is now being torn apart by a nation like Russia and this is something that is very concerning to me, as I know it is very concerning to you all.

I would like to stress what was said earlier about the support for Radio Free Europe. I think that is also very important and I hope in Congress we consider that when we are dealing with our budget priorities.

I also would like to mention just the issue of Georgia and what has been going on there and put a plug in for NATO enlargement. I think when we deal with the membership action plan for Georgia as NATO comes together, I hope they will consider putting Georgia in that.

I don't think Georgia is asking for, you know, Article 5 protection, but at least to get them on the track of understanding that America stands with its friends.

What I would like to actually really touch on and hopefully I won't take all 5 minutes, in 2011, France agreed to sell Russia two amphibious assault warships. It was a deal worth about $1.5 billion.

In fact, the Russians said that they needed this capacity because, quote—I guess, kind of quote, in the war in Georgia they were unable to control the Black Sea like they really wanted to.

So they signed this deal with the French to buy these ships called the Mistrals and it is the first-ever sale of a significant offensive military capability by a NATO member to Russia.

The first of these ships is scheduled to be delivered at the end of this year. In fact, I believe that Russian Marines are going to be coming to France to, in fact, train on these in the middle of this time, which is actually kind of shocking to me.

In light of the U.S. decision to suspend exports that could strengthen the Russian military, does the U.S. believe that France should or will proceed with the delivery of these assault ships?

Ms. NULAND. Congressman, we have regularly and consistently expressed our concerns about this sale even before we had the latest Russian actions and we will continue to do so.

Mr. KINZINGER. Okay. I think it is important just to mention on that that, again, at a time when we are looking at what is happening, I would hope the French—I understand the economic pressure and I am not here to bash the French.

But I think this is a time when the French could stop that sale from happening and send a very strong message to the Russians and, in fact, I intend to pursue this issue and continue to bring it to the attention of the American people, the administration, everyone else. So thank you for your support on that.

Mr. Chairman, I don't have a whole lot else. I am sure much of the—many of the issues were touched so I would like to yield back the remaining 2 minutes.

Chairman ROYCE. We thank the gentleman from Illinois and we go to Lois Frankel of Florida.

Ms. FRANKEL. Thank you, Mr. Chair, and I was very honored to travel with you to Ukraine a couple weeks ago and I want to thank the staff for their great work and also our State Department that helped us over there.

I want to—first, I just want to answer some of the—we heard some comments from some of our colleagues that somehow we forced Mr. Yanukovych out.

I will tell you what we learned. He was very corrupt. This is a man who lied, cheated, and stole from his people and really undermined his government and I think that is one of the reasons I am so happy that we have been trying to address this corruption, because that does undermine the confidence of people and sets the stage for a bully like Putin to—just to move in.

I actually, after visiting and really trying to study this, I feel—I am very appreciative of the position that our President has taken and our administration, moving carefully with economic sanctions because knowing the—how our European allies, how their economy is so interwoven with Russia and also dealing with these elections that are coming up, having fair and free elections, dealing—continuing to deal with the ethics and transparency, the corruption in Ukraine's Government and also trying to help them toward some type of energy efficiency.

With all that said, here is what I think is missing, and I know we have had some discussion here today about why we are involved with Ukraine—why this should matter. I believe it matters after being there and after studying this and I think one of our colleagues talked about the assurances we gave to Ukraine when they gave up a nuclear arsenal that they would keep their territorial integrity.

There are some other things that go with it, too—the nervousness of our NATO allies, what would happen if you had a failed state and so forth. But I would like to hear from you and I think the American public really needs to hear from our administration why it is that what is going on in Ukraine, why the Russian aggression is something that we should care about. That is question number one.

And secondly, I think it would also be important, and I would like you to give an opportunity to articulate to the American public, why it is that we have not just unilaterally tried to go in with sanctions—why it is so important to be respectful to what the—our European allies—you know, what their concerns are in this matter.

So I would like to—if you could address those two points.

Ms. NULAND. Well, apart from our long-time support for democratic peoples and governments and the right of free choice of citizens, this goes to the core of the rules of the road of the global world order, that you can't simply chop off a piece of another country by force and get away with it.

And this has been how conflicts start the world around. So it is about maintaining rule of law, maintaining democratic choice for people who want it and have struggled for it and are willing to sacrifice for it, not simply in Ukraine, but it is also about a very important piece of our 20-year project of a Europe whole, free and at peace.

And if Ukraine loses the opportunity to live freely then the borders of the free world in Europe shrink and the borders of opportunity in Europe shrink and that is difficult for us and it is difficult for our allies.

With regard to unilateral sanctions, we are always stronger when we work together because then you are sanctioning these entities not simply from the U.S. market but from the European market as well, and Russia depends 50 percent on the European market for all of its trade.

So if we don't do things together then not only are you blocking U.S. business from access to a market, you are potentially having U.S. businesses' holes backfilled by others so that is both ineffective and unfair. But on the whole, it is a matter of speaking with one voice about these rules of the road being inviolable.

Mr. GLASER. If I could just add to that answer on sanctions, I also think it is important to emphasize the U.S. has acted unilaterally and we are always prepared to act under our own authorities when we feel we need to.

President Obama, in this crisis, has signed three Executive orders authorizing sanctions and we have been implementing those Executive orders and those—that is under U.S. domestic authorities.

As Ambassador Nuland points out, as we move forward in this, we have been moving in conjunction and in coordination with the Europeans, but we are—we are acting under our own authorities and taking action as we feel necessary, as Ambassador Nuland points out, especially as we move to the next phase of sanctions, which could more broadly impact sectors of the Russian economy.

It is important that we are even more on the same page with our European counterparts and that is what we are doing precisely because the economies are so integrated.

But we are—we are prepared to work with our European allies to do exactly what we need to input significant costs on the Russian economy.

Ms. FRANKEL. Thank you. Mr. Royce, may I just follow up on that?

Chairman ROYCE. Yes, you certainly may, Ms. Frankel.

Ms. FRANKEL. I would just say and then—and then there were none here. You know what I think would also help for us to understand is what are the implications to the European economy with these sanctions and why do we have to be careful?

Ms. NULAND. I would just say broadly and then invite Assistant Secretary Glaser, we need—we need to ensure—different European economies are more exposed, more vulnerable in different sectors.

So as we look at sectoral sanctions we are looking at sharing the burden across sectors so no one European country is more impacted than another. That is one thing.

And then some of them are vastly energy dependent, some of them up to 100 percent, on Russian energy. So they worry about retaliation. They worry about other vulnerabilities.

And the last thing is, of course, as you know European economies are just starting to grow again after 5 years of recession. So we don't want to throw them back into that.

Mr. GLASER. I thought that was very well said. I don't have anything to add.

Ms. FRANKEL. Thank you, Mr. Chair, and I yield back.

Chairman ROYCE. Ms. Frankel, thank you. We are going to go now to Mr. Scott Perry of Pennsylvania.

Mr. PERRY. Thank you, Mr. Chairman, and thank you, folks, for your testimony. Phase three of the European phased adaptive approach envisions the deployment of the AEGIS Ballistic Missile Defense System and advanced SM–3 Interceptors, which Poland agreed to host in 2009 to counter short-, medium- and intermediate-range missile threats.

Some folks around town here are calling for the deployment of this system to be sped up. I am just asking—I want to ask what practical challenges are there, if any, to accelerating the deployment of missile defense to Poland, and is this something that the administration is pursuing or considering pursuing?

Ms. NULAND. Again, I would defer to the Missile Defense Agency for a technical answer. But my understanding is it would be considerably more expensive and there are technical challenges we haven't overcome if we were to try to accelerate.

So there would be money that would have to go into technology and money that would have to go into speeding up the timetable. I think we are comfortable that the phase two and phase three are coming online as the threat develops just to remind that is designed not with Russia in mind, but with threats from Iran and elsewhere to the south.

Mr. PERRY. So those technical questions—are they technical between the two countries or technical to the systems themselves, as far as you know?

Ms. NULAND. My understanding and, again, I haven't wonked out on this in a long time—my understanding is that it goes to the technical readiness of the system inside the United States.

Mr. PERRY. Okay. Moving on, I am wondering if exporting LNG to Ukraine and Central Europe would be a prudent response to what is happening currently and just what your thoughts on it as far as America increasing or working to increase or having a policy and a policy statement and kind of a public statement in that regard, to what effect that would be and if that is something that the administration is interested in pursuing—in pursuing an answer to what is currently occurring.

Ms. NULAND. Well, certainly, as you know, we were already working intensively with Europe to energize, if you will, their internal energy market to encourage them to make the investments in interconnectors and efficiencies in LNG terminals to allow a more dynamic cheaper market where Gazprom has to compete.

Some of that is taking place through the third energy package. In terms of the immediate Ukrainian need, our primary focus is on reverse flow energy from Europe, reverse gas into Ukraine. We have a new agreement now between brokered—that we helped broker between Slovakia and Ukraine that is going to get gas flowing reverse.

Also Poland and Hungary are pushing gas into Ukraine. Over the medium-term, we have U.S. companies investing in shale gas in Ukraine and that has the potential to make them energy independent as soon as 8 to 10 years. With regard to U.S. exports, there is quite a lot of U.S. LNG on the market.

It is going to Asia, though, because the price is higher. So here, again, we have to create more opportunities and more dynamism in the European market as the best way for both Ukraine and other countries of Europe to resist monopoly pricing by Gazprom.

Mr. PERRY. So the exports—the American exports that are currently going to Asia because the price is higher would it be—is it reasonable to say that if we produce more, exported more that the world market would then be able—the price would come down because there is more—you know, supply would be higher and then make the viability of Ukraine receiving or Western Europe receiving some American LNG more viable?

Ms. NULAND. Sorry. The most expedient thing that we could do to create a more vibrant LNG market across the Atlantic would be to complete work on our transatlantic trade and investment partnership agreement—the U.S. trade agreement with the EU—because once you are a preferential trade partner you have—you go to the head of the queue, if you will.

Mr. PERRY. And I would agree with you on that. But so there is no viewpoint from the administration that increasing or setting the table from a policy standpoint to increase LNG exports from America is part of that equation, devoid of those other things that we already discussed?

Ms. NULAND. Again, I think the President spoke about this quite a bit when he was in Europe and I am also not an LNG wonk. But he spoke about the fact that there is currently a lot of LNG coming from the U.S. on the world market but we need to continue to look at it.

Chairman ROYCE. If the gentleman would yield.

Mr. PERRY. Yes, Mr. Chairman.

Chairman ROYCE. There is some LNG coming on to the market from the United States but we have a glut on our market here in the United States.

We have the capacity—at least in speaking to the representative of the LNG facility in Louisiana we have the capacity to export into the market in Eastern Europe. By the end of the year we will have receipt facilities in place in Lithuania and Poland that are currently being built.

The question is since the shipment of gas into those markets would represent additional export of gas and given the attitudes of the administration on fossil fuels can we get the administration out front on an initiative which is the request by the government in Ukraine. The President—Acting President spoke to this issue. The Prime Minister spoke to this issue.

I think most of the Presidential candidates we met with spoke to this issue. They are desirous of a commitment by the United States to ship gas to Ukraine and it can be done through Poland, of course, now that the—now that the pipes have been reverse engineered. The administration seems to be on the other side of this argument.

Certainly, we have had the initiative in the Energy and Power Subcommittee and then the full committee on this issue that is coming before the floor and Congress will probably force this issue, just as it has the question of the Keystone pipeline, another example where the administration has stood, because of its position on fossil fuels, against importing that asset into the United States.

So I think what we are seeing is just an opposition to this policy based upon opposition to gas being a fossil fuel. We spent an hour talking with the Vice President about a number of issues in Kiev.

One of the ones we raised was trying to solicit his support for breaking the opposition and allowing—to breaking the opposition to exportive gas and incorporating that into sort of an encompassing strategy that includes the very components that Ambassador Nuland spoke to but including in that the exportive gas, which is the prime interest of the government in Ukraine, the government in Ukraine making the point that the reason they are in this situation now is because they were whipsawed on the issue of gas by Russia and that was manipulated to create the crisis, in their view anyway, inside the country that led to the current situation.

So their point is when Russia has the monopoly and when the United States doesn't announce a policy to come in and directly compete with that and drive down those prices and make this available, especially given the cooperation of Poland and Lithuania in trying to solve this equation, we are compounding the problem. So that was a big element of our discussions there.

We now go to Mr. Doug Collins of Georgia.

Mr. COLLINS. Thank you, Mr. Chairman. As, obviously, the last participant it looks like here today most of this has been discussed. I think one of the concerns is I know in talking to other members and the member from Pennsylvania we all share as one who has served and look at the issue of why we are here.

I mean, we can get into the specifics, you know, is sanctions working and I do believe that we are being too reactive in this regard, Madam Ambassador, to say that we are reactive and I know we have the issues of European nations that are concerned.

But at the same point, if we continue to back off their reserves are not going to stop Russia and Putin from doing this. I think it is sort of a false argument here as we look at it.

So my question is is we have been, I think, frankly, too reactive to the situations as a whole and not active enough. We do see them working. Iran sanctions work. They got to the table although I think they should have been in Kiev. That is not your area.

Help me out here. What brought us to this in a sense of after it has happened and now do you believe we are being too reactive? Was it prior policies that have led Russia to given the fact that they think they can do this now?

I would like to hear your just thoughts more on a 30,000 foot level and not the—you know, the tactical level. I want to see your strategic level about where you believe what brought us to this point.

Ms. NULAND. Well, that would probably be an 8-hour lunch which we could—we could have at some point. I think there are a lot of factors here including Putin's own view of lost empire, his view of opportunity, his need for an external adventure to mask problems at home.

Mr. COLLINS. Madam Ambassador, I don't mean to interrupt here. But you brought up a great point there and like I said if, you know, have a discussion over, you know, a cup of—a glass of tea would be great.

But you brought up something. We have known who Mr. Putin is. He is not a secret. He never has been a secret in his thoughts, his mind set, his whole thoughts.

And then with us pulling back from missile defense, with us doing other things in Eastern Europe, I am wondering—and frankly, I am of the opinion that some of those actually gave—in a reactive way we reacted around the world gave an empowering sense to one who does have illusions of the former empire.

I believe we have just been too reactive here and I know there is the concerns of Eastern Europe. There is the concerns of others, and I know it is not in your place to say yes, we have been too reactive.

But in this discussion I think you would at least acknowledge that that has to be part of the equation that we have to deal with going forward here and should we be as reactive as we are and not be proactive because these same countries right now that are scared of their—of their gas content and their relationship with Russia will be the same ones that turn to us if something else happens.

Ms. NULAND. Congressman, I think that speaks to exactly the kind of deterrent that we have to put forward. That is why in the NATO context for the NATO space this reassurance mission where we are doubling down on land, sea and air we have to make it absolutely clear we will defend our own space.

But it also speaks to this issue of agreeing with the Europeans as we did last week that if he disrupts these elections sectoral sanctions will be triggered as compared to where we were a month before which was that sectoral would be triggered by Russian forces coming over the border.

We now see that he doesn't need to come over the border to upset. So we are continuing to re-evaluate. But it also speaks to doing the hard work that we are doing now to develop a clear demonstrable sectoral package that he can see, that he knows what it triggers as a deterrent and to be ready if we have to use it.

Mr. COLLINS. I am very concerned though he does not know the triggers because what we have done is we have set these sort of guidelines for it and then we react. Well, we put sanctions in and then we react.

And even with this agreement, you know, in looking with the other European nations if he does this, well, you just said he didn't have to cross the border to cause chaos right now.

So is that the trigger? I mean, are we—are we making—are we setting ourselves up to say well, the trigger is he crossed the border instead of saying the trigger is he is causing internal chaos in the Ukraine.

Why is that not the discussion? Why are we limiting ourselves to a singular kind of focus instead of saying well, it doesn't matter if you cross the border—you are causing chaos in the country? That should be the trigger. Why are we, again, still very reactive, in my opinion?

Ms. NULAND. Well, Congressman, as you know, the last round of sanctions, which was about a week and a half ago, was precisely in response to the fact that we went to Geneva, we had an agreement on everybody supporting de-escalation and the Russians did nothing thereafter.

And therefore we hit seven more people. We hit 17 entities. We blocked U.S. export of high technology in the defense sector. So as we work to build the sectoral package there is also more head room in this category of sanctions that we will continue to use if necessary.

Mr. COLLINS. Okay. Well, again, thank you all for sitting through all of this. It is always, I am sure, fun for you all to come up here and discuss and get many questions.

I appreciate your answers and I would like to see a little more aggressiveness in this because, like I said, we are dealing with a man who does have—he is not an unknown quantity. It is not like he all of a sudden came out of nowhere and went to power.

We know his background and it is just very concerning to me that we are not a little more—because like I said, the Eastern European countries will be the very ones who will turn to us in a heartbeat if they are in trouble, irregardless of economic issues.

So I do appreciate you both. Thank you so much for your time.

Chairman ROYCE. Thank you. Thank you. And I—let us thank both the witnesses here. Ambassador Nuland, Mr. Glaser, thank you very much for your testimony. One of the key points that was reinforced in this hearing was the central importance of the May 25th elections.

Those elections will be a watershed in Ukraine's history. The United States must do all it can to make certain that they are fair, they are free and that people can safely get to the ballot box to cast their ballot in those elections.

It is also clear that we need a more active and long-term strategy to undermine Russia's ability to use its oil and gas exports to coerce Ukraine. When they can turn off the gas in the dead of winter, when they get that choke hold over a regime—over a government in Ukraine, you can—you can see the consequences.

So that is going to require the administration to end the sanctions that we have imposed upon ourselves. It is one thing to impose sanctions on Iran. It is another thing to impose gas and oil sanctions on the U.S. and not allow us, at a time when we have got a glut on the gas market, to put forward a strategy that will help our balance of payments, help our exports, and undermine Russia's monopoly in Eastern Europe.

And lastly, I think we must also ramp up our international broadcasting efforts to counter Russia's propaganda. Only when the people of Ukraine and the region as a whole have access to objective information will democracy and peace have a chance to flourish there.

Again, I thank our witnesses and the members, and we stand adjourned.

[Whereupon, at 12:50 p.m., the committee adjourned.]

APPENDIX

Material Submitted for the Record

FULL COMMITTEE HEARING NOTICE
COMMITTEE ON FOREIGN AFFAIRS
U.S. HOUSE OF REPRESENTATIVES
WASHINGTON, DC 20515-6128

Edward R. Royce (R-CA), Chairman

May 8, 2014

TO: MEMBERS OF THE COMMITTEE ON FOREIGN AFFAIRS

You are respectfully requested to attend an OPEN hearing of the Committee on Foreign Affairs, to be held in Room 2172 of the Rayburn House Office Building (and available live on the Committee website at http://www.ForeignAffairs.house.gov):

DATE: Thursday, May 8, 2014

TIME: 10:00 a.m.

SUBJECT: Russia's Destabilization of Ukraine

WITNESSES: The Honorable Victoria Nuland
Assistant Secretary
Bureau of European and Eurasian Affairs
U.S. Department of State

The Honorable Daniel Glaser
Assistant Secretary
Office of Terrorism and Financial Intelligence
U.S. Department of the Treasury

By Direction of the Chairman

The Committee on Foreign Affairs seeks to make its facilities accessible to persons with disabilities. If you are in need of special accommodations, please call 202/225-5021 at least four business days in advance of the event, whenever practicable. Questions with regard to special accommodations in general (including availability of Committee materials in alternative formats and assistive listening devices) may be directed to the Committee.

COMMITTEE ON FOREIGN AFFAIRS
MINUTES OF FULL COMMITTEE HEARING

Day____*Thursday*____Date_____*05/08/14*_____Room_____*2172*_____

Starting Time __*10:10 a.m.*__ Ending Time __*12:50 p.m.*__

Recesses __*0*__ (____to ____) (____to ____) (____to ____) (____to ____) (____to ____) (____to ____)

Presiding Member(s)

Edward R. Royce, Chairman
Rep. Rohrabacher, Rep. Ros-Lehtinen, Rep. Yoho

Check all of the following that apply:

Open Session ☑   Electronically Recorded (taped) ☑
Executive (closed) Session ☐   Stenographic Record ☑
Televised ☑

TITLE OF HEARING:

Russia's Destabilization of Ukraine

COMMITTEE MEMBERS PRESENT:

See Attendance Sheet.

NON-COMMITTEE MEMBERS PRESENT:

None.

HEARING WITNESSES: Same as meeting notice attached? Yes ☑ No ☐
(If "no", please list below and include title, agency, department, or organization.)

STATEMENTS FOR THE RECORD: *(List any statements submitted for the record.)*

Connolly

TIME SCHEDULED TO RECONVENE _____
or
TIME ADJOURNED *12:50 p.m.*

Edward Burrier, Deputy Staff Director

HOUSE COMMITTEE ON FOREIGN AFFAIRS
FULL COMMITTEE HEARING

PRESENT	MEMBER	PRESENT	MEMBER
X	Edward R. Royce, CA	X	Eliot L. Engel, NY
X	Christopher H. Smith, NJ		Eni F.H. Faleomavaega, AS
X	Ileana Ros-Lehtinen, FL	X	Brad Sherman, CA
X	Dana Rohrabacher, CA	X	Gregory W. Meeks, NY
X	Steve Chabot, OH	X	Albio Sires, NJ
X	Joe Wilson, SC	X	Gerald E. Connolly, VA
	Michael T. McCaul, TX	X	Theodore E. Deutch, FL
X	Ted Poe, TX		Brian Higgins, NY
X	Matt Salmon, AZ	X	Karen Bass, CA
	Tom Marino, PA	X	William Keating, MA
	Jeff Duncan, SC	X	David Cicilline, RI
X	Adam Kinzinger, IL		Alan Grayson, FL
X	Mo Brooks, AL	X	Juan Vargas, CA
X	Tom Cotton, AR	X	Bradley S. Schneider, IL
X	Paul Cook, CA	X	Joseph P. Kennedy III, MA
	George Holding, NC	X	Ami Bera, CA
	Randy K. Weber, Sr., TX	X	Alan S. Lowenthal, CA
X	Scott Perry, PA	X	Grace Meng, NY
	Steve Stockman, TX	X	Lois Frankel, FL
X	Ron DeSantis, FL	X	Tulsi Gabbard, HI
X	Doug Collins, GA	X	Joaquin Castro, TX
X	Mark Meadows, NC		
X	Ted S. Yoho, FL		
X	Luke Messer, IN		

Questions for the Record
Submitted by the Honorable Steve Stockman
To Assistant Secretary Victoria Nuland

Question1:

The current developments in Ukraine point to the importance of the principle of territorial integrity for the stability of the international legal order.

It is very concerning that Russia uses and supports separatist movements in Nagorno Karabakh, South Ossetia, Abkhazia, Transnistria and now Crimea to leverage former Soviet republics, hinder their integration to the Euro-Atlantic institutions, and eventually force them to join a Soviet-type Russia-led bloc. To counter that, the USA should consistently stand for the territorial integrity of our partners in this region and provide them with necessary support against Russian pressure.

Our consistency in upholding the principle of territorial integrity is crucial to make it credible.

Given all these, what actions is the Administration taking to counter Russian policies to undermine sovereignty and territorial integrity of our important partners like Ukraine, Georgia, Azerbaijan and Moldova?

Answer:

The United States stands firmly against Russia's continued illegal intervention in Ukraine and provocative acts that undermine Ukraine's democracy and threaten its security, stability, sovereignty, and territorial integrity. Russia's involvement in the recent violence in eastern Ukraine is indisputable. We continue to call on Russia to halt the flow of weapons and fighters across the Russia-Ukraine border, and to use its influence with separatists to urge them to cease their violent activities, lay down their arms, and abandon government facilities.

Despite provocations and violence, millions of Ukrainians went to the polls throughout the country on May 25 to participate in the presidential election and freely choose their future together. The United States looks forward to working with President-Elect Poroshenko and Ukraine's democratically elected parliament to bolster Ukraine's sovereignty and territorial integrity and to support important economic and political reform efforts.

The United States is supporting Ukraine with financial, technical and security assistance. More broadly, we are playing a key role in NATO's reassurance efforts for the eastern Allies, and we are providing support to other "front-line" states like Moldova and Georgia. Through three rounds of sanctions, we have been steadily raising the economic costs for Russia's occupation and attempted annexation of Crimea and its continuing efforts to destabilize eastern Ukraine. We are working with Ukraine and our international partners to leave the door open for diplomatic de-escalation should Russia change course and make a serious effort toward a peaceful solution.

President Obama has made U.S. support for Ukraine an urgent priority, as the Ukrainian government works to establish security and stability, pursue democratic elections and constitutional reform, revive its economy, and ensure government institutions are transparent and accountable to the Ukrainian people. The Department is grateful for the strong bipartisan cooperation we have received from Congress during this difficult period, including Congress' rapid authorization of a $1 billion loan guarantee.

Beyond the loan guarantee, we are adjusting our existing assistance programs and putting additional resources towards helping Ukraine implement these challenging economic reforms, withstand potential energy and trade pressure from Russia, and increase our support for their institutional competencies in areas such as constitutional reform and reducing corruption. On April 21, Vice President Biden announced in Kyiv a package of assistance totaling $50 million to address urgent needs in the areas of security, economic stabilization, asset recovery and anti-corruption, elections, and trade diversification. Our support also included assistance to allow the Ukrainian Armed Forces and State Border Guard Service to fulfill their core security missions.

We similarly stand in support of Moldova's and Georgia's territorial integrity. We are helping the government of Moldova secure its borders through a $35 million Defense Threat Reduction Agency program to improve the capacity of Moldova's border guard and help protect against smuggling of illicit nuclear/radiological materials. We are increasing engagement with ethnic minorities, helping to ensure access to equitable social benefits and economic opportunities, and promoting the concept of a multi-ethnic Moldova as a key to its prosperity. To counter Russian economic pressure, including the recent ban on Moldovan wine, we have increased our assistance to Moldovan entrepreneurs to enhance their competitiveness and facilitate their access to new markets. We are also continuing to provide assistance on energy efficiency and regulatory reform to accelerate Moldova's interconnection with the European energy market in order to enhance Moldova's energy security.

The United States is also an active participant in the 5+2 negotiations, which seeks to negotiate a comprehensive settlement to Moldova's "frozen conflict" with its Transnistria region, i.e., one that affirms Moldova's sovereignty and territorial integrity, while providing a special status for Transnistria. We are further working with the OSCE to get Russia to fulfill its commitments and remove its troops from Moldova's Transnistria region.

As a participant in the Geneva International Discussions on the conflict in Georgia, we are working to hold Russia to its 2008 ceasefire commitments, improve the security situation on the administrative boundary lines, and address the humanitarian needs of people living in conflict-affected areas. We are also providing Georgia with additional assistance of $1.5 million to help support Georgia's European and Euro-Atlantic vision; specifically, to help Georgia achieve visa-free travel with the EU. A key element of our assistance to Georgia has been aimed at mitigating the hardships caused by Russia's attempts to harden the borders along the occupied territories of South Ossetia and Abkhazia. The United States also is providing equipment and training to the Georgian Armed Forces to promote their reform, modernization, and interoperability with NATO and other international coalition peacekeeping forces.

Russian leverage over Armenia last year led to Armenia's abrupt turn away from a free trade agreement with the EU and towards joining Russia's customs union. Azerbaijan also experiences pressure from Russia, but its energy independence has somewhat increased its ability to act separately from Russian influence. Beginning two decades ago, the United States assisted Azerbaijan in building a pipeline to send oil to the Mediterranean, and we have long supported the Southern Gas Corridor project to bring Azeri gas to Europe through a non-Russian pipeline.

As a co-chair of the OSCE Minsk Group, the United States is working constantly to help the sides reach a durable and peaceful settlement to the Nagorno-Karabakh conflict. We continue to work with the leaders of Armenia and Azerbaijan and the de facto authorities in Nagorno-Karabakh to find a way forward in the peace process, and we support programs that bring young people and civil society together to facilitate dialogue and advocate for peace.

Regarding the conflicts involving Georgia, Moldova, and Ukraine, the United States has called on Russia and all parties to respect the principle of territorial integrity and resolve disputes regarding borders diplomatically, without recourse to violence or economic coercion. Russia's removal of its troops from Ukraine, Georgia, and Moldova is essential to restore the territorial integrity of those countries and to uphold the principles of international law. The United States is committed to working with the international community to achieve just and lasting resolutions to such conflicts.

Question 2:

Given the recent shift in the calculus of energy security for Europe with the Russian annexation of Crimea and threat to cut off natural gas to Europe, what is the State Department doing to encourage, promote, or facilitate the expedited export of natural gas to our European allies from our energy allies, including Azerbaijan, which is currently working to complete the Southern Gas Corridor that will provide natural gas to Europe upon completion?

Answer:

The Administration takes the energy security of our friends in Europe very seriously and will continue to work with the European Union (EU), bilateral partners and the G7, international financial institutions, and the private sector to map out diplomatic, energy, and market strategies to enhance collective energy security so that no nation can use energy as a political weapon. Any disruption of Russia's energy shipments to Ukraine and Europe is a lose-lose situation, with Russia losing out the most. Russia is heavily dependent on Europe and Ukraine as critical export markets for its natural gas, earning some $50 billion per year.

We support Europe in its pursuit of geographical diversity in energy sources and suppliers, increased production of both renewables and hydrocarbons, modernization of its nuclear programs, and enhanced energy efficiency, all while pursuing greater integration of the European energy market. Through the U.S.-EU Energy Council, we are working in lock-step with European partners to help Ukraine bring in natural gas from Poland and Hungary. On April 28 Slovakia and Ukraine signed an MOU for reverse flow which will initially provide up to 3 bcm of capacity annually, but with work could provide up to 10 bcm of capacity in the future. We also support the Southern Gas Corridor, a pipeline system that will deliver Azeri Caspian Sea natural gas through Turkey into Greece and on to Italy. Last year, after more than a decade of U.S.-led energy diplomacy, a final investment decision was made on this pipeline, which will bring 10 billion cubic meters (bcm) of natural gas from Azerbaijan to southern Europe starting in 2019.

In terms of the energy security implications of U.S. exports, we must be mindful that energy markets are complicated and change in these markets is a more long-term proposition. The Department of Energy (DOE) has regulatory authority over permits for Liquefied Natural Gas (LNG) exports and has already conditionally approved LNG export permits for 9.3 billion cubic feet per day (or 96 bcm per year) that can be exported both to countries with which we have Free Trade Agreements (FTA) and to those where we do not, such as European countries. The first project to export this gas is expected to come online in late 2015. Approved LNG exports are significant. To put it in perspective, 96 bcm per year is more than the total amount of LNG Europe currently imports and equal to over half the gas Europe imports from Russia. We are committed to putting gas onto the global market in a way that is consistent with U.S. public interest because increased global supplies help our European allies and other strategic partners.

Questions for the Record
Submitted by the Honorable Brad Sherman
To Assistant Secretary Victoria Nuland

Question:

On the question of when and why the U.S. supports territorial integrity over self-determination around the world, you indicated that the use of violence by a state against a minority is perhaps the prominent factor in U.S. support for self-determination for that minority. If so, how do you explain the U.S. position on the Republic of Biafra in the late 1960s? How do we deal with the question of Eritrea and Ethiopia's territorial conflict?

Answer:

Both of these conflicts occurred within the broader context of the Cold War, which shaped every aspect of American foreign relations through that period. American policy with respect to the secession of Biafra from Nigeria was further influenced by the secessionist movements in the Congo in the early 1960s, which had triggered a devastating war, a major confrontation between the United States and the Soviet Union, and a protracted humanitarian crisis.

The Kennedy/Johnson administration had dealt with that crisis since their first days in office, and as a result maintained a steadfast policy with respect to Nigeria in the late 1960s. A Department cable to the embassy in Lagos summarized the situation: "USG seeks maintain Nigerian unity because it realizes East's defection would cause grave problems for rest of country as well as for East and because prospects for further fragmentation would be high." The Department was focused on maintaining a unified Nigeria, and equally on averting violence by any of the players, under the expectation that "Resort to force, regardless of which army...won battles, would set off tribal violence in many parts of Nigeria, but particularly in Lagos area which still harbours mixture tribal people....Consequence of this tribal violence rather than clash between armies would almost certainly lead to breakup of Nigeria into at least three new countries." As the political system in Nigeria disintegrated, Secretary Dean Rusk and the American embassy in Lagos made it clear to the secessionist leaders that they could expect neither recognition nor support from the United States – an effort by the Administration to deter a breakup. Beyond intensive bilateral diplomatic efforts, the Administration supported and instigated a series of attempts at mediating the conflict by African leaders.

While maintaining this policy, the Administration judged that the internal composition of Nigeria was, in the end, a matter for the Nigerians to decide. An NSC staff memo a few days before Biafra's secession summarized the situation: "My own considered judgment is that no foreign power can assert anything like decisive influence on the Nigerian situation without commitment of major resources – troops and money. On balance, I *don't* think it is worth such a commitment on our part... The truth is... we don't have the bilateral tools to affect the outcome. We can marginally influence the *method* of change – particularly, I hope, limit violence— but the unity question is beyond us." The United States attempted to restrict the scale of violence, risking the relationship with Nigeria by limiting arms and ammunition sales at the outset of the conflict. Over time, as the Nigerian government gradually gained the advantage in the war, the Nixon Administration conducted a significant humanitarian effort in Biafra to help ameliorate the costs of a protracted, brutal war – exactly the type of situation the U.S. had attempted to avert.

U.S. policy with respect to the Ethiopia-Eritrea conflict more directly reflected the Cold War context. Ethiopia was considered a major geopolitical asset, both with respect to its position on the Horn of Africa, and in hosting a major communications site at Kagnew. Emperor Haile Selassie had been an American hero since Ethiopia's war with Italy before World War II, and the United States had long nurtured a "special relationship" with His Imperial Majesty. The United States supported that relationship with economic and military aid beginning in the mid-1950s. A Department cable to the embassy in Addis Ababa in April 1964 summarized the bilateral relationship as perceived by American policy makers: "Ethiopia remains largest recipient US military aid in Africa. This, we believe, indicates importance we attach to Ethiopia as major factor working for African stability and as symbol African responsibility." Accordingly, as the Eritrean conflict began in the early 1960s, the United States was far more concerned with Ethiopia's recurrent clashes with Somalia – seeking to preserve Ethiopia's security, contain the conflict, and restrain Ethiopia from taking offensive action into Somalia.

Among other concerns, the Department was concerned that ongoing violence would create an opening for Soviet diplomacy on the Horn of Africa; in early 1964, for example, the Department noted to the embassy in Addis Ababa that "Sov Dep Foreign Minister Malik's second visit Addis Ababa in slightly over a month and two Khrushchev letters to Emperor Selassie on Ethiopian-Somali dispute within roughly same period underscore Moscow's effort to play "peacemaker" and exercise predominant influence in Horn of Africa." Under these circumstances it was unthinkable that the United States would support an Eritrean secessionist movement that would break up Ethiopia and destroy the long-standing relationship with Selassie.

This steadfast American support for Ethiopia changed rapidly with the coup that deposed Selassie in September 1974, eventually leading to a remarkable swap of allies between the Soviet Union and the United States during the Carter Administration – the Soviets moving toward support of Ethiopia, and the United States taking up support of Somalia. The Carter Administration paid close attention to the Horn of Africa, deeply concerned about the Soviet Union's increasing presence there and throughout the continent. Its priorities were directed toward limiting Soviet influence and preserving America's position, within a general context of deterioration in the détente relationship, and the rapid growth of Soviet military power and reach.

Finally, it is important to note that neither of these secessionist movements enjoyed significant support among other newly independent African states. Because African territorial boundaries were defined by the European colonial powers without any regard for self-determination or any naturally unifying force such as language or race, every country has the potential for secession movements. When the Organization for African Unity (OAU) was formed in 1963, respect for territorial integrity was one of its main tenets and considered most important by African leaders. U.S. support for any separatist movement would have been enormously unpopular with the rest of the continent.

Statement for the Record
Submitted by the Honorable Gerald Connolly

The situation in Ukraine has taken a grave turn for the worse in recent days. We are witnessing open and armed clashes in the streets and pro-Russian militants are usurping the authority of local governments. Militias supposedly constituted solely by civilians have shot down 3 Ukrainian military helicopters, and on May 11, the separatist-run Donetsk People's Republic will hold a referendum on the region's sovereignty similar to the illegitimate referendum used to establish Crimea's independence.

President Vladimir Putin would have us believe that Russia has lost control over the pro-Russian militants taking up arms against their government in eastern Ukraine. The Russian President made this claim after 50 people were killed during the deadliest day in Ukraine since February.

I am not sure which part of the Russian President's assertion is more unbelievable; that Russia openly admits to seeding the destabilization of a sovereign nation or that Russia contends that the situation in eastern Ukraine is beyond the purview of its control and influence. The Russian President cannot reasonably expect the world to divorce Russian intervention from the violence we are seeing in Ukraine. Russia's repeated attempts to undermine the sovereign governments of former Soviet Republics by stoking the discontent of ethnic minorities now constitute Russia's *modus operandi* on foreign subterfuge.[1]

In Georgia, Moldova and now in Ukraine, Russia has claimed a national prerogative to interject itself into the domestic affairs of former Soviet Republics under the guise of minority rights. Russia fine-tuned this model early in the post-Cold War era. In 1992, it supported the armed resistance of separatists in the Transnistria region of Moldova and the South Ossetia and Abkhazia regions of Georgia. It has since used a steady stream of trade sanctions and involvement in domestic opposition movements to foment unrest and instability in former satellite states. At times, the resulting domestic strife has escalated into Russian military aggression as it did in Georgia in 2008 and as is currently the situation in Ukraine.

For countries seeking to shed authoritarian institutions, Western economic prosperity and democratic freedoms can be like a moth to flame. Cold War era geopolitics dictated that the endgame for the USSR was to extinguish that flame. In the post-Cold War era, Russia has its sights set on the moth.

For the sake of American diplomacy, I hope we have clarity about our role going forward. On March 27, the House of Representatives took one step in the right direction when it passed H.R. 4278 by a 393-19 vote. The legislation, which imposed economic sanctions on Russia and authorized loan guarantees and direct aid for Ukraine, was to this end.

The legislation included my amendment that requires the State Department to issue an annual report on: an assessment of the security situation in regions neighboring Russia, including Crimea; the goals and factors shaping the security strategy of the Government of Russia, including potential annexation of non-Russian territory; trends in Russian security behavior that would be designed to achieve Russia's security goals; an assessment of the global and regional security objectives of Russia that would affect NATO, the Middle East, or the People's Republic of China; an assessment of the capabilities of Russia's military, and those capabilities' effects on Russia's neighbors; and any other developments that the Secretary of State considers important to national security.

The violence in Ukraine and other former Soviet Republics brings Russian aggression to the world's attention. I hope our witnesses can provide guidance on how the U.S. intends to leverage this attention, how it is reshaping U.S. post-Cold War diplomacy in Eurasia, and shed light on regions that are currently simmering but could easily boil over with the help of Russian provocation.

---

[1] "Russia's Latest Land Grab." Foreign Affairs. 17 Apr. 2014. Web. 6 May 2014.
<http://www.foreignaffairs.com/articles/141210/jeffrey-mankoff/russias-latest-land-grab>.